D0602399

MAKE IT
WITH
PAPER

MAKE IT
WITH
PAPER

THE WELLFLEET PRESS

WELLFLEET

A QUINTET BOOK

Published by Wellfleet Press
110 Enterprise Avenue
Secaucus, New Jersey 07094

Copyright © 1992 Quintet Publishing Limited.
All rights reserved. No part of this publication
may be reproduced, stored in a retrieval system
or transmitted in any form or by any means,
electronic, mechanical, photocopying,
recording or otherwise, without the permission
of the copyright holder.

ISBN 1-55521-803-2

This book was designed and produced by
Quintet Publishing Limited
6 Blundell Street
London N7 9BH

Creative Director: Peter Bridgewater
Art Directors: Pete Laws, Ian Hunt
Designers: Annie Moss, Linda Henley
Editors: Barbara Fuller, Sandy Shepherd,
Judith Simons
Illustrators: David Kemp, Lorraine Harrison
Photographers: Ian Howes, Andrew Sydenham
Stylists: Paul Jackson, Vivien Frank

The material in this book previously appeared in
Classic Origami and *Origami and Papercraft.*

Typeset in Great Britain by
Central Southern Typesetters, Eastbourne
Manufacturered in Hong Kong by
Regent Publishing Services Limited
Printed in Singapore by Star Standard Industries Pte. Ltd.

CONTENTS

Paper is one of Man's greatest inventions. Think how many times a day you use it as writing paper, wallpaper, tissues, banknotes, newspapers, books, magazines, envelopes, packaging, tickets, photographs, cheques, computer print-outs — the list is almost endless.

Think also of how many times a day you throw paper away. That list too is almost endless. We see it as a short-lasting, everyday material to be used and discarded. But think again!

For arts and crafts, paper is the most versatile of all materials. There are thousands of different papers in an enormous range of colours, weights and textures. Paper is readily available, usually inexpensive, simple to store and requires the help of only the most basic materials and equipment, such as scissors or glue, to transform it into any number of beautiful objects. Sometimes, as in origami, only the paper itself is used.

What's more, the variety of papercrafts is such that whether you like to make things that are decorative, practical, ingenious, geometric or expressive, there is bound to be one craft that will appeal to you.

The projects inside have been chosen to show the diversity of papercrafts. They are divided loosely into two sections: the first shows how you can give a sheet of paper an interesting surface, either by making your own paper or by decorating existing sheets; the second introduces some three-dimensional papercrafts, such as serviette folding, papier mâché, pop-ups, boxes and bags, or paper flowers.

We, the authors, hope that our enthusiasm for all things paper will inspire you to make some of the projects, and that they will give you pleasure and satisfaction.

Paul Jackson

Vivien Frank

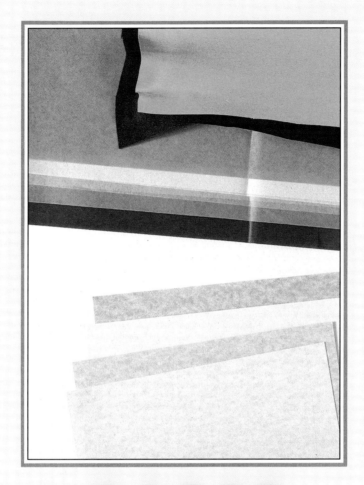

PAPER
AND
EQUIPMENT

Page 7 Top Crêpe and double crêpe papers are forms of tissue paper which have been passed through a patterned roller when wet; this gives them their characteristic crinkled and stretchy qualities.

Page 7 Bottom Textured papers. The texture is printed on and gives a soft looking, rich surface, although not as vibrant as patterned papers.

Bottom left Decorated origami and gift-wrapping papers are printed as part of their manufacturing process. Some are printed on one side only, which increases their versatility in papercrafts.

There are three types of paper: handmade, mould-made and machinemade and paper has two basic and important qualities – weight and grain. Handmade papers, which often incorporate long fibres, have no grain (the direction in which the fibres lie) and have four deckle edges (a deckle is the rough edge of the paper). Mouldmade papers are less expensive than handmade ones and are made by machine, but have two deckle edges and longer fibres than those used in machine-made papers. Mouldmade and machinemade papers both have a grain.

Other terms which are often used when talking about paper are "laid", "wove" and "sized". "Laid" paper is made on a mould which has wire, or sometimes wooden, bars laid across the frame. These bars allow a thinner deposit of pulp to be laid and leave an impression in the sheet of paper. This impression may be visible only against the light. Watermarks are formed in the same way. Paper without these lines is called "wove", from the woven mesh on which the pulp is poured. Paper can be "sized", which means that it is coated with a glue substance (usually gelatine or starch), or it can be "unsized". Sized paper is less absorbent than unsized and therefore ink or paint do not bleed when drawn or painted on it. Unsized paper is known as "waterleaf".

PAPER WEIGHT

Paper is often measured by grammes per square metre, referred to as g/m^2 or gsm^2. Where the weight of paper is given in pounds, it refers to pounds per ream (a ream is 500 sheets, whatever the sheet dimensions). It is possible to convert pounds per ream to grammes per square metre but it is rarely necessary.

An average paper, such as writing paper, weighs between 80 and 120 gsm^2. Tissue and Japanese papers are obviously much lighter. Paper weighing more than 225 gsm^2 is card; it becomes board when it weighs 500 gsm^2 and more. To complicate matters further, card and board are also measured in micrometres, which indicates their thickness.

PAPER GRAIN

The grain of paper is pronounced in machinemade papers because the mould on which they are made is a moving belt and the fibres settle in the direction of the movement of the belt. This grain can be used to advantage in that paper will fold, curve, tear and crease more easily along its grain. But it also has disadvantages: when wetted, as in glueing, the fibres swell widthways but not lengthways, and although they compress again when dry, if two surfaces are being joined, you may end up with a curved surface. To avoid this, try dampening both sheets of paper.

To find out which way the grain runs in a piece of paper, curl the paper in both directions and, while pressing gently with one hand, feel which way bends more easily. Another way, although somewhat extravagant, is to tear two strips from the paper, one in each direction. When you are tearing with the grain, the tear will be much cleaner and less irregular. There is also grain in card and board; discover this by flexing the sheet between your hands and then turning it through 90° and flexing it the other way; it will flex more readily in the direction of the grain.

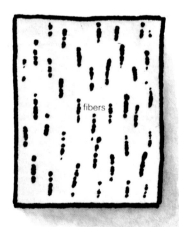

1 A sheet of paper with the grain running from top to bottom.

2 The sheet will bend easily when the lefthand edge is brought over to the right, because the bend follows the direction of the grain.

3 The sheet will not bend as easily when the top edge is brought down to the bottom, because the bend runs across the direction of the grain.

4 A torn edge is straighter when it follows the direction of the grain than when it runs across the grain.

Below Lightweight card has many uses, from making templates to small boxes. Heavier card and corrugated paper can be used for packaging or surface decoration.

Right Foil papers are made by coating paper with adhesive and then with coloured metal powders, which are then burnished. Embossing is often applied to metallic foils backed with paper, as here. This is done by running paper between rollers which have been engraved with a pattern.

Left Ingres (or Strathmore) papers are often recognizable from their uneven surface appearance with visible hair-like fibres. They are lightweight to mediumweight papers.

Left Gift-wrap papers come in a huge range of patterns and textures and are printed onto white paper. The reverse is left unprinted. They are invaluable when decorative effects are needed.

Above Marbled papers are formed by laying coloured oil-based inks onto water. Paper is laid on top and then removed, pulling the inks with it. The best examples are marbled by hand, although cheaper printed sheets can also be purchased.

Left Japanese papers are often extremely fine in appearance, but because they are made with long fibres, they are usually very strong.

Left Handmade papers are the most beautiful of all papers. Their surfaces are rich in colour and texture and will make any papercrafts project look extra special.

Left Coloured papers and card come in a wide range of weights and colours and are an attractive alternative or contrast to white.

CRAFT EQUIPMENT

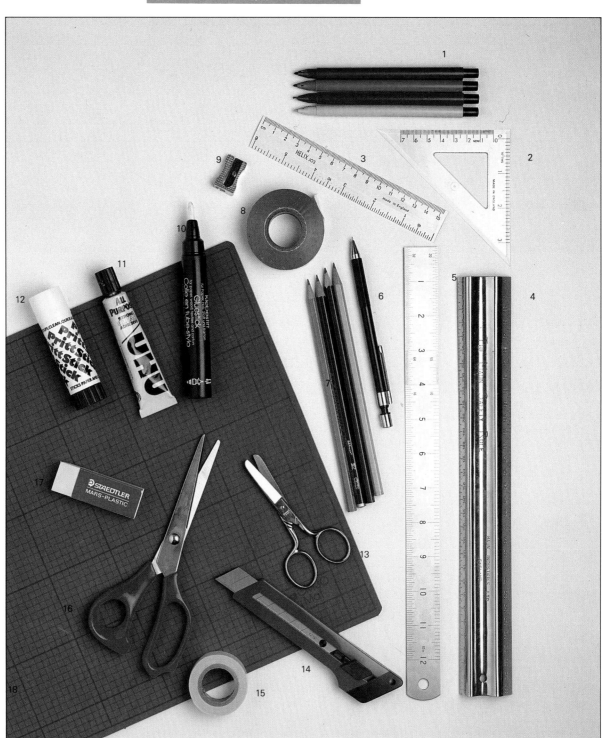

1 Felt-tipped pens
2 45° triangle
3 Small plastic ruler
4 "M"-shaped safety
   ruler
5 Metal cutting ruler
6 Automatic feed pencil
7 Graphite pencils
8 Clear adhesive tape
9 Pencil sharpener
10 Glue stick
11 Clear adhesive
12 PVA adhesive
13 Round-tipped craft
   scissors
14 Retractable craft knife
   with snap-off blade
15 Double-sided adhesive
   tape
16 Scissors
17 Vinyl eraser
18 Self-healing cutting mat

MAKING
PAPER

MOULD-AND-DECKLE METHOD

For most of its 2,000-year history, paper has been made by hand. However, since the Industrial Revolution in the late 18th century and the invention of machinery that could mass-produce paper, the craft has become a highly sophisticated industrial science. Yet making paper is essentially a simple process and one which is tremendous fun and surprisingly creative. It is a craft in which all the family can participate – even young children can make their own sheets of paper.

Traditionally, handmade paper is made from hemp or, more commonly, from recycled cotton rags. Both substances have unusually long fibres, which bind together well in the papermaking process to form a strong material. To make these fibres into paper they have to be broken down and separated, which means boiling them in caustic substances. To keep the method practical enough for you to try in your own kitchen, this chapter will deal only with recycling existing papers. Quite a few books have been written in recent years which explain how to make paper from plant fibres, so if you get the bug, look for them in your local library or bookshop.

SUITABLE PAPERS FOR RECYCLING

The best papers for making good white sheets include unprinted computer paper, typing paper, writing paper and photocopier paper. Other good, but more unusual, papers include Ingres (Strathmore) paper (all weights), cartridge or drawing paper, watercolour paper, card, printed computer paper and old novels or picture books printed on good-quality paper. Even tissues, serviettes and tea bags can be used. To help soften thicker papers and card, soak them overnight before blending them (see below).

Avoid using newspapers: they are made from cheap poor-quality pulp which has a high acid content and turns brown very quickly. Also, avoid shiny papers such as china paper and glossy magazine paper: they are coated with china clay, which turns to a crumbly powder when recycled. Poster paper and other papers coated with a coloured pigment should also not be used. If in doubt, always try out a paper. In truth, very few types are unsuitable for recycling.

Above Here are just a few examples of the many effects of colour, texture and design that guarantee making paper at home is such fun.

This method makes thick sheets of paper because the deckle frame traps a lot of pulp on top of the mould. For thinner sheets, add extra water to the pulp.

EQUIPMENT

- Paper to be recycled.
- A blender. One with a 2 pint/1 litre/4 cup capacity jug is the best, but any size will do. Paper is not poisonous, so rest assured that the jug will not be contaminated.
- At least one large, oblong mashing-up bowl. Circular or oval ones are the wrong shape. Make sure they are very clean, or unwanted particles of dirt will appear in the paper pulp.
- An old bath towel to cut up, capillary matting (available from plant nurseries) or any other very absorbent material.
- Smooth, all-purpose, striped viscose kitchen cleaning cloths (you will need one for each sheet of paper). Don't use coarse cloths because they texture the paper when it is pressed, unless, of course, you want this texture.
- Plenty of clean newspaper, preferably broadsheet (large format), which has not been folded into quarters. If possible, start collecting well ahead of making paper because you will need a lot.
- Two sturdy wooden boards about 12 × 18 in (30 × 46 cm). The boards need not be identical or clean, but the wood must be strong enough not to bend, so don't use hardboard (Masonite) or thin plywood.
- A palette knife.
- A few heavy books or other weighty objects.
- A large flat surface to work on.
- Plastic sheeting, refuse bags or a waterproof table-cloth to cover the work surface and nearby carpets.
- A sink.

EQUIPMENT

1 Large oblong bowl
2 Two wooden boards
3 Two wooden frames (see page 18)
4 Blender
5 Plastic sheeting
6 Large format newspapers
7 Curtain netting (see page 18)
8 Old bath towel
9 Palette knife
10 Viscose kitchen cleaning cloths
11 Paper for recycling

MAKING A MOULD AND DECKLE

You will need a mould and deckle on which to deposit the wet pulp before it is pressed and dried to become paper. They can be bought in craft shops or by mail from craft suppliers, but it is easy enough to make your own. If you have enough materials, it is well worth making a few sets of moulds and deckles.

2 Pin the curtain netting over the top face of one frame. A constant tension of net is important, so first pin it to the middle of one outside edge, then to the middle of the opposite outside edge, pulling it reasonably tight. Pin the middles of the two remaining outside edges, then begin to work towards the corners, pulling the net reasonably tight and pinning it as you go.

EQUIPMENT

Enough ¾ in (2 cm) square wood to cut four 8 in (20 cm) lengths and four 5 in (12.5 cm) lengths

Plain curtain netting or similar open-weave fabric. The size of the mesh is not critical, but should not be too tight or too open

Drawing pins (thumb tacks)

Eight "L"-shaped brass plates (with screws), not wider than the wood

A screwdriver

1 Cut the wood to the lengths described above, and arrange them to make two identical frames. Let the ends of the short lengths touch the sides of the long lengths. Screw the brass plates to the corners of one face only, to hold the frames together. Alternatively, if you have the equipment and necessary carpentry skills, mitre the corners, apply a waterproof adhesive and nail them together.

3 To complete, fold over the net at the corners to make a neat finish. Trim off the excess net. This frame is the mould, and the uncovered one the deckle.

The mould and deckle can be made much larger, but you will not be able to use them in a bowl. A baby bath is a good alternative.

PREPARING THE PULP

The pulp can be prepared in advance and can be done by young children who greatly enjoy ripping paper to shreds! Tear several layers of paper at once to speed the process.

BLENDING TIMES

As a rough guide, blend computer, photocopy, typing, writing and similar papers for 25–35 seconds, cartridge (drawing) paper and Ingres (or Strathmore) papers for 40–50 seconds, tissue for 60 seconds and card for 70–90 seconds (less if previously soaked overnight in water). The result should be a thin fibrous soup. If globules of fibre are still coagulating, blend for a little longer. If the machine is labouring, take out some of the paper. Do not be tempted to overload the jug.

1 Tear (never cut) the paper to be recycled into pieces about the size of large postage stamps. Fill the blender no more than three-quarters full of water and put in no more than 35 torn pieces of paper for every 2 pints/1 litre/4 cups of water. Switch the blender on.

2 Pour the pulp into the washing-up bowl. Repeat the blending process until the bowl is half to two-thirds full, but not brimming over.

FORMING THE SHEET

Stir the pulp gently with your hand to distribute the fibres evenly in the water. Unstirred, they soon settle to the bottom. Repeat this every time the pulp is left to stand for more than a few minutes. This agitation is an important part of the process: be careful not to forget it as it will affect the success of this project.

1 Fit the deckle exactly over the mould, so that the brass plates on the deckle are on the top surface away from the mould, and the net on the mould rests against the deckle in the middle of the "sandwich".

2 Hold the long edges of the mould and deckle together tightly at the far end of the bowl, making sure that the deckle is facing you.

3 Then, with smooth movements, lower the short edges of the mould and deckle vertically into the pulp.

4 Pull the mould and deckle towards you while at the same time bringing them to a horizontal position under the pulp, with the deckle on top of the mould.

5 Lift the mould and deckle straight out of the pulp, being careful to keep them horizontal. Hold them a few inches above the pulp and let the excess water drain through at the same time shaking them gently backwards and forwards, left and right, to help the fibres settle evenly on the net as the water drains.

6 Rest two adjacent edges of the mould on the nearside corner of the bowl.

7 Support the underside of the mould with one hand, and with the other, lift off the deckle quickly. Be careful not to drag the deckle into the pulp on the net, or it will damage the edge of the paper. Also avoid letting water drip off the deckle onto the pulp.

8 The pulp is now reading for couching.

COUCHING

This is a traditional term for transferring wet pulp from the mould onto the sheet of material on which it will dry. Before forming the sheet of wet pulp on the mould, prepare a couching mound. Make this from an old bath towel which has been cut up, capillary matting, or other very absorbent material.

1 Cut up the material to make a small mound the same shape and size as the mould. Wet it to help it lie flat. (Take some time to do this properly.)

2 Cover the mound with a damp, all-purpose, striped viscose kitchen cleaning cloth, so that the nearside short edge of the cloth just covers the nearside edge of the mound.

3 To form the wet pulp on the mound, rest the long edge of the mould on the cloth 1 in (2.5 cm) in front of the foot of the mound, so that the pulp is on the far side of the mould, facing the mound. Hold as shown.

4 In as fluent a movement as possible, lower the sides of the mould gradually onto the mound, pressing firmly.

5 Lift the bottom edge off the cloth, pushing the top edge firmly into the cloth.

6 The pulp should stick to the cloth. If it doesn't, this is probably because the mound is too tall, too flat or has the wrong dimensions.

Experiment with its shape until the pulp couches satisfactorily. Alternatively, the cloth may be too dry; wet it again.

7 Fold the remainder of the cloth over the sheet of pulp. Be very careful not to leave any creases in the cloth where it covers the pulp, or they will be moulded into the sheet when it is pressed, spoiling its smooth surface.

8 Lay a second damp cloth over the first and couch another sheet onto it as described above. Fold the cloth in half as before.

9 The process can be repeated a dozen times or more, each new sheet being couched on top of the others in a growing pile. Don't forget to lay out a new damp cloth for every sheet so that each is in its own folded cloth "sandwich".

PRESSING

The method described here looks very rough and ready (it is!), but works extremely well. A more professional way would be to use a proper paper press. They are, however, quite expensive and difficult to find.

CAUTION!!

Unless you have a waste-disposal unit, when you empty the bowl of pulp at the end of a paper-making session, do not pour it down a sink. The fibres will congeal in the sump, causing a blockage. Instead, sieve the pulp through a strainer so that the water drains into the sink. Put the dough-like pulp that has remained in the sieve into the dustbin, or use it to make a deckle-only sheet of paper (see below).

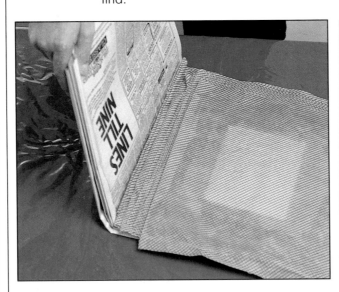

1 Put the pile of couched sheets onto one half of the back page of a broadsheet (large format) newspaper. Fold the other half of the newspaper over the pile, sandwiching the sheets in the middle.

2 Put the sandwich between two sturdy wooden boards.

3 Stand on the boards for about two minutes, squeezing out most of the water from the cloths. The heavier you are the better. This is best done out of doors, because a surprising amount of water will come out. Alternatively, do it on a bathroom floor or other tiled floor which can be mopped dry.

DRYING

This is the stage which is easiest to rush, but you must be patient. Let the paper dry at its own pace. Attempts to speed the process by ironing the paper or placing it near a heater may "cockle" (warp) it.

1 Remove the pile of damp cloths from the sodden newspaper. Take a new, dry newspaper and turn over three sheets to pages six and seven. Lay out two cloths on page six, then turn over three more sheets, covering the cloths, and lay out two more cloths on page twelve.

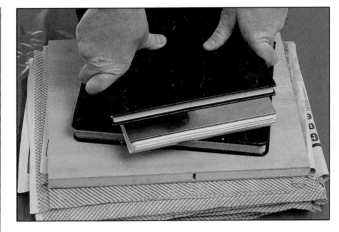

2 Put the newspapers back between the boards and weight them with a few large books or other objects of a similar weight.

After about two hours, remove the cloths from the newspapers and lay them out as before into fresh newspapers. Once again weight them between the boards and leave for a few hours. Repeat the laying-out process every six hours or so until the cloths and handmade paper are completely dry. This may take a day or more, depending on how thick the paper is and how much water it held originally.

3 When the paper is completely dry, open the cloths and gently slip a palette knife under the edge of the paper. Move it slowly under the sheet all round in a sequence of slicing movements, separating the paper delicately from the cloth. It is possible to do this with an ordinary kitchen knife, but a palette knife is easier to use and kinder to the paper, particularly if it is thin.

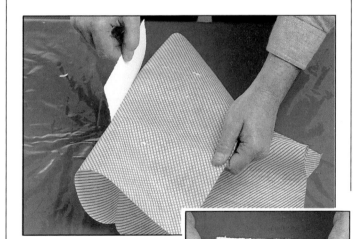

4 Hold an edge of the paper and peel off the cloth. Do not hold the cloth and pull the paper off because this will bend the paper and possibly damage it. The paper is now finished (**right**).

OTHER METHODS

THE MOULD-ONLY METHOD

The mould-and-deckle method but without the deckle will produce a thinner sheet because the absence of a deckle means that less pulp is held on the mould.

Use the mould without the deckle to produce finer sheets. If the pulp is already watery, the sheets formed using this process will be extremely thin and beautifully delicate.

SIZING

This process is necessary to stop inks and paints from bleeding into paper when they are written or drawn on. Unsized paper acts like blotting paper, diffusing a line of colour, though this can sometimes be an attractive effect.

To size a sheet, simply add two teaspoons of coldwater starch to the bowl of pulp. Stir it and carry on making the paper as before. If you want a smooth writing surface, press the sheets with a medium-cool iron when they are nearly dry. Never iron the paper directly, but do it through a layer of fabric.

THE DECKLE-ONLY METHOD

This is a rough-and-ready method for making paper, or at least a fibrous mat, without the need for a net stretched over the deckle.

1 Blend the pulp for about one-third longer than the usual time, then pour it through a sieve. The water will drain away to leave a thick dough-like pulp trapped in the sieve.

2 Lay out a damp kitchen cloth and place a deckle onto one half of it. Empty the contents of the sieve into the frame and spread it about evenly to make a pulp mat. Sieve as much pulp as is needed to form a mat ¼–½ in (6–12 mm) thick. If you have a pipette or turkey baster to hand, squirt some thin pulp onto the mat to help it bind.

3 Remove the deckle and fold the remainder of the cloth over the pulp. Press and dry as described for the mould-and-deckle method.

CREATIVE EFFECTS

1 Make a bowl of white pulp. Blend a small quantity of orange paper in a little water for about 10 seconds, so that it is not quite pulped, but shredded into small speckled pieces, and pour it into the white pulp.

2 Repeat the previous step with a similar quantity of grey paper.

3 Form the sheet on the mould as before (with or without a deckle), then couch, press and dry. The sheet will be white with orange and grey speckles.

SPECKLED SHEETS

You may think, and with reason, that it is a little odd to tear up a piece of paper, only to reconstitute it so that it looks pretty much the same at the end as it did at the beginning!

If these are your thoughts, look at the following creative suggestions. It is at this point that papermaking becomes an open-ended art form, where the only limitation is your imagination. Assume no rules, no right or wrong, just enjoy it. You will be surprised how often a silly idea, or indeed a silly mistake, can give a beautiful result.

4 Try speckling the paper with white speckles in a coloured pulp, or with any other combination of colours. As an alternative, blend tea leaves in a little water and add them to a white or coloured pulp. You could also add small objects directly to the pulp without blending them: seeds, short lengths of hair or coloured threads, confetti, small scraps of fabric, colourful flower petals or autumn leaves, all make an attractive effect when embedded in the paper.

LAID-ON EFFECTS

1 Couch a white sheet. Then tear up strips or cut out shapes from sheets of coloured tissue paper and lay them on top of the couched sheet. As the sheet dries, the tissue will remain stuck to it.

2 To achieve subtle coloured effects try the following method. Couch a sheet and lay paper or whatever you choose on top. Form another sheet using the mould only and couch it exactly over the top of the first sheet. This traps the coloured items between two layers of pulp, but they will still be faintly visible.

TIP

Try creating laid-on effects with thin and thick pieces of coloured paper. With thick pieces, press and dry the paper on the couched sheets, then peel it off. Some of its coloured pigment will have run off onto the main sheet to form a coloured shadow (see left). Other interesting laid-on effects can be created with tickets, wool, petals, leaves (see left), sand, etc.

SHAPED PULPS

1 Couch a white sheet and mix a bowl of coloured pulp. Hold an edge of the mould (without the deckle) and drag part of it vertically through the pulp, net side first.

2 Remove the mould from the pulp – the pulp will be deposited onto only part of the mould. Couch it over the top of the white sheet.

3 The coloured pulp will cover part of the while pulp. Press and dry as before. Various effects can be achieved (**below**).

TIPS

■ Try mixing up a few differently coloured pulps and couching them on the same sheet, or dragging a corner of the mould through the pulp, in order to change the shape of the pulp on the mould.

■ To achieve more complex shapes of coloured pulp, stick a paper shape to the top of the net, leaving holes where the pulp has to couch. Put all the mould under the pulp in the conventional manner. Pull it out and remove the paper shape, taking part of the pulp with it. Those parts of the net that were not covered with the paper will have retained pulp. Couch onto a previously couched sheet.

USES FOR HANDMADE PAPERS

Plain white sheets or sheets of a pale colour make very attractive writing paper. For thin writing paper, form the sheets on a mould without a deckle, see page 26. If you do not want the writing inks to run, remember to size the pulp, see page 26. Thicker sheets make unusual business cards, calling cards, gift tags or table place names. To form the small shapes needed for business cards, either make a very small mould and deckle, see page 18, or mask part of a larger mould with a paper shape, see page 29.

Right To make greetings cards, glue a sheet of your paper to the front of an ordinary piece of card which has already been folded down the middle. Another sheet of handmade paper, possibly plain or starched, can be glued inside the card to hold a written greeting. Perhaps the most effective use of creative papers is to assemble a patchwork of sheets and frame them. Sheets which may be considered not good enough to become greetings cards or which are too eccentric, become surprisingly attractive as a patchwork. Framed, they are always a talking point.

DECORATING
PAPER

EQUIPMENT

1 Various mediumweight
    papers
2 Adhesive tape
3 Glue stick
4 Scissors or craft knife
5 Metal ruler
6 Pencil

There is an infinite number of ways to decorate paper, some of which will be explained in this chapter. Within each method there are many variations, because the results will differ depending on the type and colour of paper used. For example, ink on tissue paper will give a very strong colour, but if you thin the ink and splatter it on a heavy, absorbent, coloured paper the effect will be much more subtle.

Some of the techniques discussed will produce finished work, and others are only a step towards a bigger project. Just the basics of each method have been explained, but hopefully your imagination will be stimulated to experiment and take them further.

WEAVING

Paper weaving can be extremely challenging but can also be very simple. It can be used in a purely decorative way to make a picture or in a more practical way to form a box. The pleasure comes in the many exciting types and colours of paper you choose to use for your efforts. The main thing to remember is that there are no rules and the experimenting is all part of the fun. The paper used can be coloured, patterned or textured, and even illustrations from magazines.

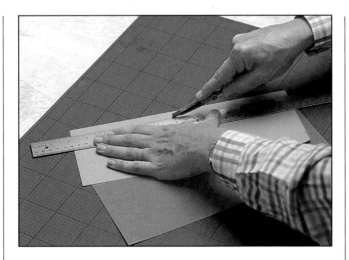

1 Using a metal ruler and a craft knife, cut strips of paper. These will provide straight edges in the pattern. Use a variety of colours, if desired.

2 Alternatively, tear strips to create a looser-edged pattern. Use different colours for greater effect.

3 When you are combining strips of paper in a woven design, the vertical strips represent the "warp" threads and the horizontal strips the "weft" threads, as in any form of weaving. Cut the warp into zigzags and thread different coloured and textured strips through it.

4 Alternatively, cut the warp into curves for a wavy pattern and thread different-coloured weft strips through it.

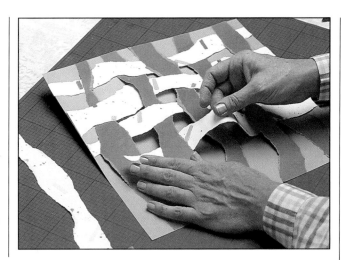

5 For a more random effect, tear the strips and lay them across and through each other. The warp can be spread out and the weft can be woven irregularly so that spaces show between the strips.

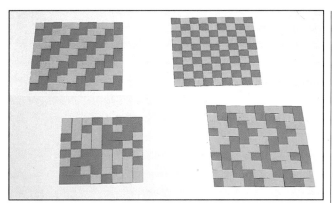

Above Rigid, geometric patterns are produced with straight-edged strips.

Right Create interesting patterns with irregular warp and weft strips.

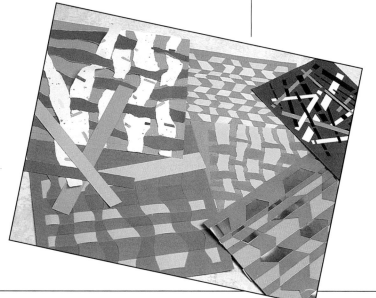

COLLAGE

1 Lightweight to medium-weight paper
2 Coloured tissue paper
3 Japanese papers
4 Glue stick or spray adhesive
5 Gummed papers
6 Foil papers
7 Decorated adhesive tape
8 Self-adhesive stickers

The word collage comes from the French verb *"coller"*, meaning "to stick". Collage is regarded as an art form and the examples shown here can be developed further.

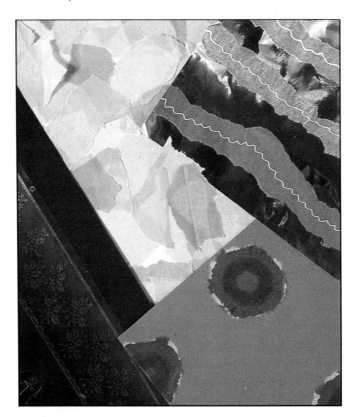

Remember that the dyes used in tissue paper are not usually colour-fast, so take this into account when you are using different colours: yellow and purple may look nice next to each other, but mixed together the result will be a murky brown!!

Left These finished examples can be used for many of the projects covered later in the book.

■ Although expensive, decorative Japanese papers can also be used to great effect.
■ If time is short or you do not feel very creative, make decorative patterns by covering plain papers with bought stickers or sticky patterned tapes, or with your own shapes cut out from pre-gummed papers.

1 Tear up small pieces of tissue paper and place on glued lightweight paper, using spray adhesive or a glue stick.

2 Leave some edges of the tissue paper unattached and allow them to overlap a little. Finished sheets can be cut up and used on the front of a greetings card, see pages 84 and 85.

STENCILLING

1 Mediumweight paper
2 Stencil paper
3 Self-adhesive shapes
4 Foil
5 Spray diffuser
6 Toothbrush
7 Stencil brush
8 Sponge
9 Paint brush
10 Paints and paint palette
11 Coloured inks, felt-tipped pens and coloured pencils

Below and below right Fold a sheet of paper and cut or tear shapes out of the folded edges. Colour through or round the shapes onto another piece of paper.

Above Cut shapes out from stencil paper. Both the negative and positive parts of the stencil can be used.

Stencilling can be messy, so it is advisable to protect the working area and surrounding surfaces with newspaper to avoid accidents. The patterns in this section are mostly created by blocking out an area of paper and colouring the remaining part. The blocking out can be done using several kinds of stencils.

Try using self-adhesive shapes as stencils. Paint over them and then remove when dry.

Cut shapes out of a folded sheet of foil. Unfold the shape and brush one colour through it. Swivel the stencil round slightly and paint through it with another colour to create an attractive kaleidoscopic effect.

If you apply the colour with a sponge, some of the cellular texture of the sponge will transfer onto the paper. For an even effect, use a spray can or airbrush. For a fine stippled effect splatter the paint onto the paper from a toothbrush or a larger brush. Dip the brush in the liquid paint and shake off the excess before drawing a finger or ruler across the bristles. Keep the bristles facing downwards!

You can apply colour in a number of ways. Try brushing the colour on with an ordinary paint brush, or for a more stippled texture, use a stencil brush.

STENCILLING TIPS

▌ Spray the paper with water first before you stencil onto it, to increase its absorbency; the colours will spread more when you apply the paint.

▌ Do not make the paint too wet or it will run under the edge of the stencil.

▌ Do not load too much colouring medium on the brush or sponge, or the texture of the mark will be lost.

▌ Folded paper stencils cannot be used too often because they absorb the paint and become too sodden to be used cleanly.

▌ When using self-adhesive shapes, allow them to dry before you remove them to make sure that you do not smudge any part of the design.

▌ Try using acetate as a stencil material, and cut it with a scalpel or craft knife. As it does not tear, this material allows for quite a lot of detail and also has the advantage of being transparent so it can be positioned exactly with ease.

▌ Try tearing a large shape from a piece of paper and place it on another sheet; paint over the edges all around the shape. Lift off and tear off the painted edge, making the shape smaller and changing it slightly. Reposition it within the painted area and, perhaps with another colour, paint over the new edge. Repeat the same process as many times as possible.

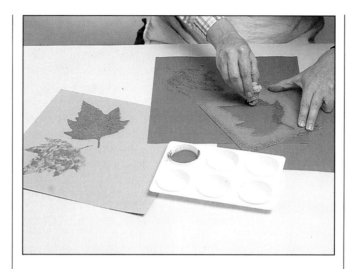

1 Using a leaf-shaped positive stencil, paint is applied to a coloured background with a sponge.

2 Using the cut-out leaf shape as a negative stencil, paint around the shape with a stencil brush.

3 You can have great fun experimenting with these methods. Try using several colours in one design, or use coloured paper as the background, as this will add to the design.

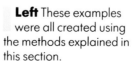

Left These examples were all created using the methods explained in this section.

RESIST METHODS

EQUIPMENT

1 Wax crayons
2 Wallpaper paste
3 Wax candles
4 Poster (alkyd) paints
5 Bowl
6 Wide brush
7 Black drawing ink
8 Mediumweight to heavy-
   weight paper

These methods can be tightly controlled or very random. They can be done with wax crayons and paint, wax rubbings and paint, paste and paint, or wax crayons and ink. Wax crayons and paint and wax rubbings and paint are very similar in application, although the final result is very different in that the first can be used to create a picture, whereas the second produces a pattern. Paste and paint is not strictly a resist method, but the end result looks similar to other resist methods. It is a good way of making textured patterns on paper.

WAX RUBBINGS AND PAINT

1 Cover a textured surface, such as a strip of plastic netting, with a piece of white or coloured mediumweight paper and rub a candle or coloured wax crayon over the paper. Remove it from the textured surface.

3 Make sure that you brush the paint right over the edges of the paper, and protect the surrounding area with waste paper. Allow the paper to dry naturally.

2 Next, brush some thin water-based paint over the entire sheet. The paint can be one colour or can be brushed on in stripes of different colours.

Left These examples show a variety of rubbings on papers of different textures. Look around you for different materials which can be used for rubbings: cane chair seats, tennis racquets, brick walls, tree bark – the list is endless.

■ Mix the paint wash thinly and always mix enough to cover the whole sheet, ensuring an even tone of colour.
■ Use a wide brush to cover large areas: this will save you time and effort.
■ It is possible to use thin paper for this method. If you mount it onto another sheet of lightweight paper it will be strong enough to make a box or bag, see pages 76–86.

PASTE AND PAINT

2 Now let your imagination take over. Using a finger, the handle of a paint brush or an improvised comb (as **left**), draw patterns in the paste and paint mixture.

1 Mix wallpaper paste to the directions on the packet – it should be reasonably thick but not lumpy. Add water-based paint to this mixture. Test the intensity of the colour on a piece of paper (**top**). Using a broad brush, spread the paste mixture across the whole sheet as evenly as possible (**above**).

3 If you do not like the design, simply brush over it and start again! Depending on the amount of paste you use, the patterned paper will take quite a while to dry. To create a lighter appearance, when the paper is almost dry, lay a piece of thin paper (newsprint or similar) on top of the pasted paper and rub evenly over it, or use a roller, and then peel it off.

Right An infinite range of attractive designs can be created using different implements to pattern the paste mixture.

WAX CRAYONS AND INK

1 Using the crayons, draw bands or areas of colour on to heavyweight paper. If you would prefer a black and white design, use white candle wax on white paper. Now, paint over the entire area with black drawing ink. It may be necessary to repeat this step in order to cover the wax crayon completely.

2 When the ink is dry, take any improvised drawing tool – the handle of a paint brush, the bottom of a pencil (**above**), an empty ballpoint pen or the end of a ruler (**top**) – and scratch through the ink to reveal the colours of the crayons. Either draw a picture or make a pattern; whichever you choose the results will be stunning.

Left The four finished examples here show both random and controlled techniques.

TIP

The above process can be reversed – paint an area with black paint, and when it is dry, colour in areas over it with the wax crayons, pressing firmly onto the paint. Then scratch through the wax areas to reveal black lines or shapes, giving more detail to the crayoned design. This method creates a more individual design than the wax band of colour painted with ink.

DIPPING AND FOLDING

EQUIPMENT

1 Thin absorbent paper
2 Kitchen tissue
3 Small dishes
4 Coloured ink, food
  colouring or watercolour
  paint
5 Stiff brush
6 Bulldog clips
7 Roller

This method is simple, quick, colourful and, for these reasons, very exciting. It involves folding paper in various ways and then dipping it into a coloured liquid.

It is essential that you use very lightweight paper for this process, but you will have to experiment with different brands to discover which papers work best. For the photographed examples here, coloured tissue papers and large sheets of lens tissue, available in some specialist paper shops, have been used. Many of the tissue papers sold in packets are not colour-fast, and when they are wet their colour may run. This can add to the design, but you should be aware of this possibility. It may be advisable to wear surgical rubber gloves while working with your chosen colouring medium (household gloves are too cumbersome to enable you to unfold the wet tissue without tearing it).

TIPS

■ For softer-edged effects first dip the paper into water and squeeze it out before colouring it.
■ Be careful not to transfer any colour to the base of the iron; this is more likely to happen if the paper is still wet.

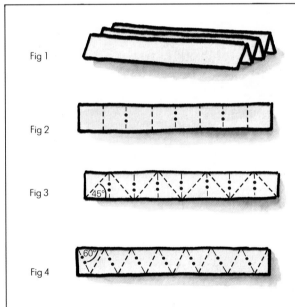

Fig 1

Fig 2

Fig 3

Fig 4

All designs start with some form of accordion pleat (see Fig 1). For dip dyeing, fold the pleat into smaller shapes (see Figs 2, 3 and 4 for some of the possibilities). The broken lines represent valley folds, or creases which recede, and the dot-and-dash lines represent mountain folds, which come forward.

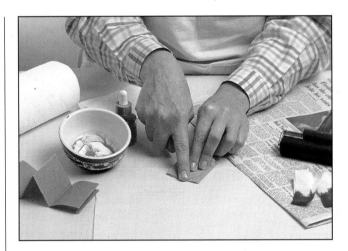

1 Make an accordion pleat (see Fig 1) with your chosen lightweight paper – coloured tissue paper is ideal. Now fold as in Fig 2, 3 or 4, or experiment with your own folding ideas.

2 Pour some colouring – liquid watercolour, coloured ink, food colouring or similar – into a shallow container (preferably one that will not stain) and dip either a corner or an edge of the folded paper into it. Allow the paper to absorb the colour and let it spread a little.

3 Squeeze the excess liquid from the paper between kitchen tissue or newsprint. Continue to colour the folded paper as much as you require. At this stage the wet tissue is very fragile.

4 Unfold the paper so that it forms a long pleated strip. Place this strip on some waste paper, cover it with more waste paper and either rub hard all along the strip or, preferably, use a roller. This removes a great deal of the excess moisture.

5 Now unfold the paper completely. Take care not to tear the tissue. Move the paper as little as possible at this stage and allow it to dry. When it is dry it can be ironed to remove some of the crease marks.

Above These dip-dyed examples show a variety of methods: use of wetted paper (left); felt pen technique (top right); wetted paper completely dyed (right); and use of dry paper (bottom right).

ALTERNATIVES

It is also possible to draw patterns into the folded shapes, using felt-tipped pens. When the paper has been folded, dip it in water and squeeze it gently so that it is damp, not dripping. The felt pens will now easily penetrate several layers of paper. Open the folds partially to check how far through the layers the colour has seeped, and rework the pattern from the faintest layer outwards. Fat felt tips give bold results, whereas fine felt tips give delicate and more detailed patterns. Dry as for the basic method already described.

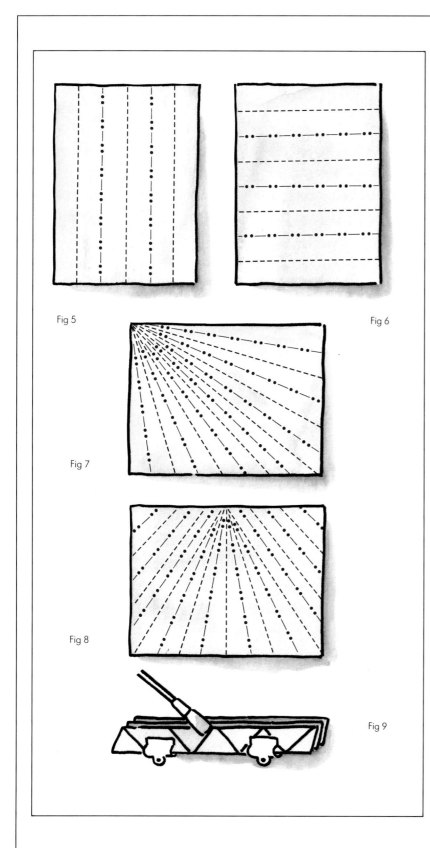

Fig 5

Fig 6

Fig 7

Fig 8

Fig 9

PLEATING

A method related to folding and dyeing is pleating and painting. There are many ways to pleat a piece of paper (see Figs 5–8 for some ideas). When the paper is pleated, hold the edges together on one side with bulldog clips, and paint the edges on the other side (see Fig 9). Repeat the process for the opposite edges. Dry as for the basic method. It is possible to repleat another design – checks or chevrons, for example – when the paper has dried, and to paint it again.

The finished papers are extremely decorative and can be used for many other projects: greetings cards, see pages 84–5; wrapping gifts, see pages 70–1; papier mâché decoration, see pages 54–6. The tissue paper can be mounted onto other sheets of paper using spray adhesive. It could be used in this form for lining envelopes, see page 86, and as a cover for a stationery holder, see pages 89–94, or a notepad.

Above These finished examples show different ways of pleating: straight pleating of coloured tissue paper (left); diagonal pleating (top right); and repleating (bottom right).

MARBLING

The technique of marbling, by which paper is given a marbled pattern, is thought to have been invented in eastern Europe in the sixteenth century. The process relies on the fact that oil and water do not mix. Oil colours are floated on size or water, the paper is laid on the surface of the liquid, and when it is lifted off, picks up the pattern of the colours. It is a simple technique but needs practice to achieve consistent patterns. However, do not be deterred because it is a most enjoyable craft to practise, and even your first experiments will be presentable.

Marbled papers are mainly associated with bookbinding, but these days they appear on many household accessories: lamps and lampshades, candlesticks, wastepaper bins, stationery holders and boxes, etc. Some marbled papers are now printed, but these do not usually have the quality – both visually and texturally – of handmade ones.

EQUIPMENT

1 Shallow tray
2 Mediumweight paper
3 Pins
4 Medicine droppers
5 Knitting needle
6 Marbling combs (see page 50)
7 Oil colours
8 Mixing jar
9 Ox-gall
10 White (mineral) spirit
11 Wallpaper paste
12 Measuring spoons
13 Measuring jug

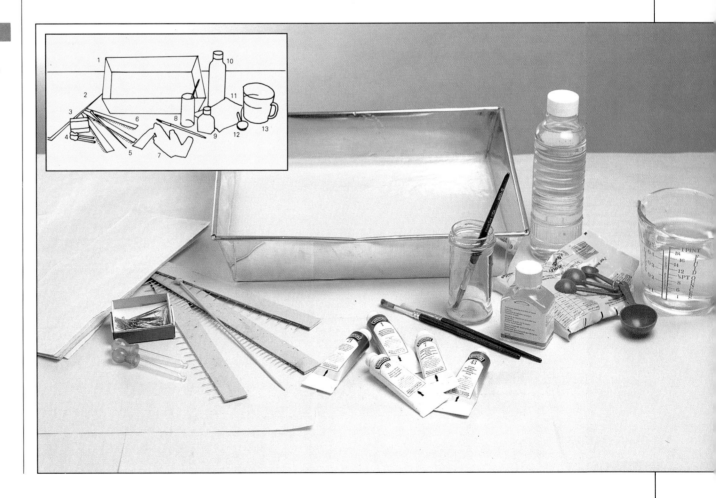

PREPARING THE BATH

Using approximately one heaped tablespoon to 2 pints/1 litre/4 cups of hand-hot water, mix about one-quarter of the water with the paste (also known as size) in the tray until the paste is smooth. Then add the rest of the water, stirring well so that the size is free of lumps. Allow the mixture to stand for a while and prepare the colours.

Marbling can be done with a single colour, particularly if you are using coloured paper, but two or three colours can also be used. Squeeze out some oil paint onto a saucer or a palette. Add some turpentine or white spirit (mineral spirit) and stir continuously until the colours are thinned to a runny consistency. Then transfer the colours to individual jars.

The next step is the most uncertain part of the process and will probably require several attempts. Add ox-gall to the colours in order to reduce the surface tension and to allow the colours to spread on the size.

Ox-gall reacts differently with each colour, depending on factors such as the temperature of the room and the size, the consistency of the colours, etc. Start by adding five drops of ox-gall to two teaspoons of each colour. If colours are being placed on top of each other, the second colour will need additional ox-gall. However, you can make these adjustments during the marbling session.

Make sure that you have plenty of strips of newspaper or newsprint prepared for skimming excess colour from the surface of the size. The strips should be slightly narrower than the tray and 3 in (7.5 cm) wide.

Having completed these basic preparations, it is now time to start experimenting with the consistencies and temperatures of the size and the oil colours. Test each colour individually (see chart) before attempting to use two colours or more together.

TEST CHART

CAUTION It is essential that you skim the surface of the size with the strips of paper between each trial so that you can see clearly how the oil colours are reacting and also to get into the habit of skimming the surface between patterns.

■ If the colour disperses too thinly, there is too much ox-gall and you will have to add more thinned colour.

■ If the colour does not spread, there is not enough ox-gall — add more, drop by drop. If this does not work, it is possible that the size is too thick and more water should be stirred in carefully.

■ If the colour sinks through the size, it usually means that the size is too thick and should therefore be thinned.

■ If the colour still sinks, the temperature of the size may not be right. If the size feels warmer than room temperature, then add cold water to it, and if it feels colder, add warm water.

Left Some decorative examples using these marbling techniques on coloured as well as white paper.

BASIC METHOD

1 Having achieved all the right consistencies, it is time to make a pattern. Drop colour randomly from a brush, loaded with colour, tapped against the side of the tray. Repeat with more colours, if desired.

2 Using a stick or knitting needle, draw patterns in the size by dragging the implement through the oil colours. Take care to work only on the surface of the size and move the pattern-making implement gently and fairly slowly so that you disturb the bath as little as possible.

3 When the pattern looks satisfactory, take a piece of lightweight to medium-weight paper by the opposite corners and lay it onto the size carefully, with a rolling movement. Do this fairly slowly or else air bubbles will become trapped beneath the paper, forming unintended white spaces in the pattern.

4 Lift off the paper almost immediately by picking up two adjacent corners and peeling it off the surface of the size.

5 Let it drain on the side of the tray for a minute or so and then lay it on some newspaper to dry. If you wish, you can rinse the paper very gently to remove the excess size, but this can affect the colour and is not really necessary. It is also possible to hang the paper on a line to dry.

DESIGN VARIATIONS
1A Drop colour onto the size with a pipette (**above**).

1b Repeat, dropping further colours onto the first colour (**above**).

1c With a knitting needle, draw through the centre of the dots to make a continuous thread (**above**).

2a Alternatively, intersperse different-coloured drops of paint on the size.

2b Draw down through the rows of dots to feather the colours and create a design.

2c Agitate the surface slightly with the needle to make the lines of colour wavy.

CAUTION!!

Remember to clean the excess colour from the surface of the size before you start to create the next pattern. Lay a sheet of clean paper onto the paste mixture to soak up any remaining colour.

2d Lay the paper slowly down onto the size.

2e Quickly lift the paper off.

3a Alternatively, use larger movements to swirl the colours.

3b This produces a bolder, spiral design.

4 Bang the 2 pieces firmly together with a hammer so that the cards are firmly stuck together. Additional combs can be made, setting different spaces for the "teeth".

HOW TO MAKE A MARBLING COMB

1 Take 2 strips of card ½ in (1 cm) shorter than the width and/or length of the tray, and about 2 in (5 cm) wide. Mark off ½ in (1 cm) spaces on 1 strip.

2 Cover the edge of the strip with double-sided adhesive tape.

3 Position long pins on the tape at the marked points. Stick more tape to the other piece of card and stick the two cards together carefully.

5 Drag the comb lightly through the colour on the size, shifting it slightly as you do so to make a wavy pattern.

PAPIER MACHE

TIPS

■ One way of keeping track of the completed layers is to use different types of paper for alternate layers – such as newspaper and coloured tissue paper. Eight layers is a good average for most articles.

■ Depending on the object, it may be wise to make the base thicker; for example, a waste-paper basket would benefit from the extra strength and weight of a thicker base.

■ The larger the article the longer it will take to dry.

The craft (some would say art) of making objects out of papier mâché is almost as old as paper-making and was first practised by the Chinese. The objects they produced were practical and decorative, and were often made especially for festivals, when they were painted with religious images. In the 18th century, papier mâché had a resurgence of popularity in Europe and was used for many household pieces, from trays and boxes to tables and chairs, which were often highly decorated. Nowadays papier mâché is frequently used for theatre props, because it is simple to construct, lightweight, and, combined with modern epoxy glues, incredibly strong.

The term *papier mâché* is French and means "chewed-up paper". This describes the process very clearly: paper is torn into small pieces, glued and laid onto a mould. Several layers of paper are built up and, when the shape is thoroughly dry, it is removed from the mould, sanded smooth and decorated.

An alternative method is to make a papier mâché pulp or mash. It is complicated to prepare, but very easy to use. However, proprietary brands are now available for home use. In this book the basic "strip and glue" method has been used.

EQUIPMENT

1 Old newspapers
2 Coloured tissue paper
3 Wallpaper paste or thinned PVA adhesive
4 A mould
5 Petroleum jelly or plastic film
6 Scissors
7 Sandpaper
8 Paint brushes
9 Undercoat
10 Decorating materials and varnish

BASIC METHOD

Prepare the working area by covering the table with newspaper. If you are using wallpaper paste, mix it according to the directions on the packet; if you are using PVA adhesive, dilute it with three parts glue to one part water.

Choose a mould with no under lip otherwise it will be impossible to remove the finished object. Now cover the mould with petroleum jelly or plastic film, so that the papier mâché object can be removed easily when the layers are dry.

1 Having torn up the newspaper and tissue, dampen the pieces, and lay neatly on the mould.

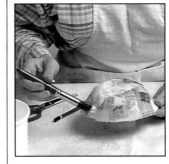

2 When the mould is covered, paint the surface liberally with the thinned adhesive or paste.

3 Now add the next layer.

4 When the mould is covered with this layer, brush on more adhesive. For a smooth result, try to work methodically so that the mould is covered evenly.

5 Put the mould in a warm place and leave it to dry for about 24 hours. Remove the shape from the mould carefully.

6 If necessary, trim the edges of the shape.

7 If the edge feels uneven or thin, it is possible to build up the shape at this stage.

8 Using medium- to fine-grade sandpaper, sand the article smooth and then paint it with two layers of undercoat. This ensures that the object has an even base on which to apply the final decoration.

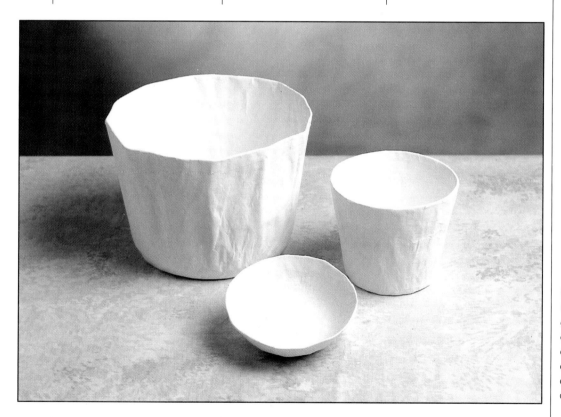

Left There are many possibilities for decorating the finished object: you could apply collage or stencil a design onto it, see pages 35–7, or draw or paint onto it directly.

DECORATING PAPIER MACHE

BOWL 1 This bowl has such an open shape that the outside is barely visible. Therefore, it is painted in a single colour and the inside is more decorative.

2 Cut a piece from a sheet of folded and dyed Japanese paper. Apply thinned PVA adhesive to the base of the bowl. Place the cutout in position and press down gently as the dye may not be permanent and may spread.

3 Cut circles from coloured tissue paper and stick them round the edge of the bowl. Again take care when sticking these in position that the colour does not run.

4 When the first layer of circles is tacky, position the smaller circles and paint over them with another layer of PVA adhesive, which acts as a varnish. It is possible to use many overlapping layers of coloured tissue and work on a coloured background, which will affect the colours of the tissue. Try out various designs, using coloured paper for experiments.

Left The finished bowl, complete with decoration, makes an attractive container.

PLANT POT HOLDER

1 The plant pot holder here has been decorated with leaf stencils. These are made from lightweight paper so that they can be curved around the shape easily and attached to the holder with small pieces of plastic putty.

2 The holder was then sprayed with another layer of paint, in a well-ventilated space. You could achieve the same effect by painting onto the object with a brush.

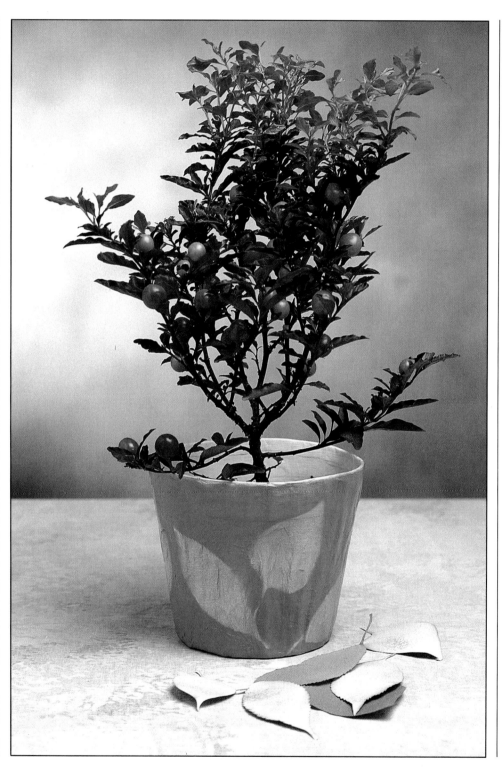

Left The stencils were then removed. The inside was left undecorated because it will be hidden by the plant. Varnish was applied to the pot holder to make it waterproof.

WASTEPAPER RECEPTACLE

1 The outside was decorated with a collage of torn paper strips of newspaper and thin black paper.

2 The strips were pasted and then positioned randomly around the shape.

3 After positioning, the strips were trimmed to fit. They were allowed to overlap at the bottom, but were cut flush at the top.

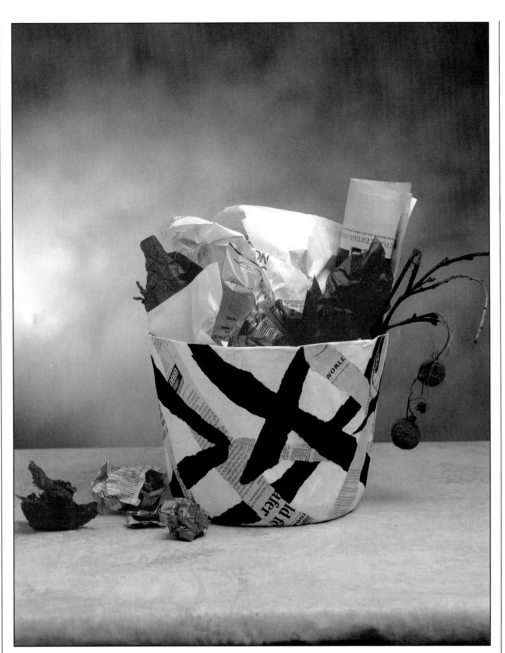

Left The inside should be varnished or covered with enamel paint. The end result is original and effective, and simply achieved.

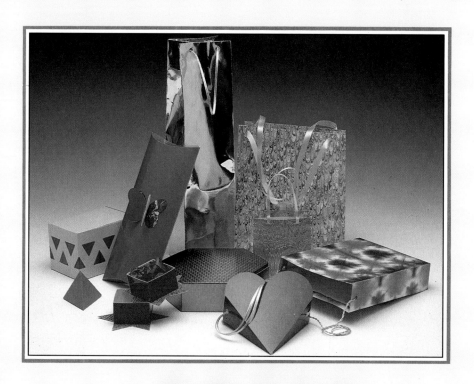

BOXES
AND BAGS

This chapter opens up almost endless possibilities and many of the ideas are asily carried out. The most inexpensive gift can be made to look very special in its own box, and gifts which are awkward to wrap effectively can have their own custom-made box or bag.

The boxes should be made from thin card and the bags from various weights of paper, see pages 8–13. If coloured card (sometimes called board or art cover board) is not available, it is possible to glue gift-wrapping paper or decorated paper, see pages 32–50, to thin card. Make sure that the grain of both the card and the paper runs in the same direction, see page 9. Apply the glue evenly, but not excessively. Press the paper to remove any air bubbles.

When cutting curves you will achieve a smoother line if you keep the scissors in the same position while closing the blades slowly together and turning the card evenly with the other hand.

Score paper and card before you fold it because this helps to create a good crease. If possible, use a bone folder; otherwise, a blunt knife or the back of a scissors blade will do. If you are using a heavyweight card it may be necessary to cut through half the thickness of the card to achieve a good fold. Do this very carefully, using a craft knife or scalpel.

In order not to be wasteful, it may be wise for you to try out the more complicated boxes using paper first, before working on an expensive sheet of card. This is also a useful way of checking that the dimensions of the box are correct for the gift that you are planning to place within it.

In all the diagrams in this chapter the solid line should be cut and the dotted lines should be scored and a broken line represents a placement line. After you have removed the shape from its sheet and scored it, remember to fold all the lines to check the angles and the fit before you do any glueing. Small adjustments can often be made at this stage.

Glue flaps are used for all the projects in this chapter. They should be at least ½ in (1 cm) deep. If the shape is large, the glue flaps could be made up to 1 in (2.5 cm) deep. Tucking flaps are used on many of the boxes; these are always a little deeper than the glue flaps and can be cut at a more oblique angle to provide a tight fit.

Below These basic boxes were made from card which had been decorated using techniques described in the Decorating chapter see pages 32–50.

BASIC BOX

When drawing a plan for a basic box, work out the dimensions and whatever the size, make sure that all angles are 90°, see Fig 1. The larger the box the thicker the card should be.

The number of flaps should equal the number of cut edges.

Use a sharp knife to cut out the shape, and cut away from the work – it would be infuriating to cut into the shape accidentally, having spent time carefully drawing it out.

Check the fit of the box, and stick the sides together, using a clear, all-purpose adhesive, rather than a glue stick. Next, stick the base in position. The box is now complete.

If you are using plain card you could decorate the outside, or cover the card with gift-wrapping paper. It is best to decorate or cover the card before assembling the box.

It is possible to make the basic box collapsible. Add the glue flaps to the base instead of the bottom of the sides, and then stick only the side glue flap in position. The box can now be flattened and assembled when required. But remember that the box will not be as strong as a rigid one and do not forget to stick the base in place so that the bottom does not fall out of the box at the wrong moment!

EQUIPMENT

1 Sharp pencil and ruler
2 Knife and metal ruler
3 Cutting mat or scrap board
4 Scissors
5 Bone folder (if possible)
6 A pair of compasses
7 Protractor and/or set squares
8 Various glues
9 Various adhesive tapes
10 Thin card
11 Paper

Above These three boxes were made from plain-coloured card with different dimensions using the basic method.

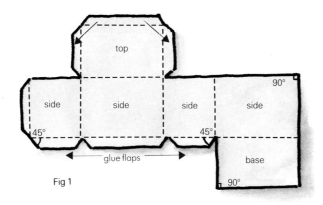

Fig 1

TWO-PIECE BOX

A two-piece box can be as simple as the silver box in the photograph, or more complicated, like the red one with the star shape. A two-piece box is more economical to make than the basic box, but cannot be collapsed.

1a The easiest way to make a box with a separate lid is to cut out the box shape to the required size and to stick the sides together, using adhesive tape (decorated adhesive tape is very effective here).

1b Make the lid in exactly the same way, but make the sides very short; the dimensions of the rectangle should be 1/16 in (1.5 mm) larger in both directions to accommodate the thickness of the card.

1c If adhesive tape is not suitable or available, the same result can be achieved by adding glue flaps. Make sure the allowance for the card thickness is generous when you are making the lid because the glue flaps will increase the thickness.

2a To make the blue box in the photograph, mark out a strip of card which is equal in length to twice the length and twice the width of the gift plus a glue flap, and equal to the height of the gift plus a glue flap. The strip can have joins if necessary. Cut out, score the folds and glue to form a box.

2b For the wrap-around lid, mark out a piece of card measuring the length of the gift by twice the width and twice the height plus an overlap. Cut out and score the folds.

2c Glue the centre section of the lid to the glue flaps at the base of the box. Fold the side and top pieces around the box, enclosing the gift. Either tie it to close or seal with a sticker.

3a To make the red star-shaped box, mark out a strip of card (see 2a), but with the sides of equal measure to form a square box. Make the lid in the same way, but slightly larger.

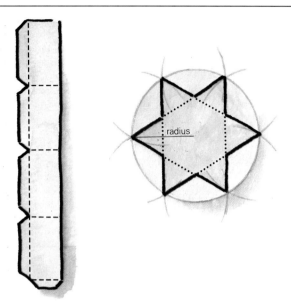

radius

3b To construct the star, measure the length of one side of the box with the compasses. This is the radius of the circle. Draw the circle. Keeping the same radius setting, place the point of the compasses on the circumference of the circle and mark the point it crosses on the curve. Move the compass to this point and repeat the process until you have six points around the circumference. Join alternate points with a pencil and ruler.

3c Cut out two star shapes and glue one to the flaps at the base of the box and the other to the flaps at the top of the lid. The box is now complete.

Left The possibilities for decorating homemade boxes are endless. Decorated adhesive tape, stickers and attractive ties all add a professional finishing touch. The basket-type box was made using metallic strips of card woven together, see pages 32–3, with a simple strip attached to act as a handle.

COVERING BOXES

Boxes can be re-used; chocolate and soap boxes particularly are often a suitable size for other gifts. There are two ways of disguising their previous uses. Often it is necessary only to re-cover the lid, but the method is the same if the bottom is also being re-covered.

1 Measure the width and length of the box lid and the height of the box sides. The piece of paper will need to be big enough for the lid measurement plus four times the sides. Draw the rectangle in the centre of a piece of lightweight paper; add sides all around and then add another set of sides to turn in. Draw "ears" as in the diagram.

2 Cut out, score and fold the whole shape. Position the box on the drawn rectangle, turn the "ears" inwards.

3 Stick the "ears" and the turn-in allowance down.

4 Then stick the opposite sides.

VARIATIONS

Many interesting patterns can be made using corrugated paper; the boxes in the photograph (**left**) show two designs. Always cut the corrugated paper with a sharp knife on the wrong (flat) side without pressing hard, because this would flatten the "ribs". Use a fairly strong adhesive. Cover the top first and then, with the covered top downwards, wrap a strip of the corrugated paper around the sides.

COMPLEX BOXES

FLAT GIFT HOLDER

This type of box is most suitable for flat gifts, such as scarves and ties. Measure the gift and then make the gift holder the length of the gift, and the width plus the height of the gift (if the gift is solid, allow a little extra). At its deepest point, the curves at the top and bottom of the holder should measure approximately twice the height of the gift.

With these measurements it is now possible to draw the plan of the gift holder, see diagram. The curve can either be drawn with the compasses, placed on the centre line, or using a dinner plate of suitable size. Join two sides with one curve and trace this off onto a piece of scrap card and use this as a template to draw the other curves. Cut out and score. Stick the glue flap to the side. Place the gift in the holder and close by turning in the curves.

To make the gift holder extra-special, a shape, a butterfly for example, can be cut and folded from the right side; stick a piece of decorative paper underneath and lift the cut-out.

Left The blue gift holder is decorated with a butterfly-shape cut out (see main text). The green one was made with lightweight card that had been decorated with a stencilled design, see pages 35–7.

Right Basic plan for the flat gift holder.

PYRAMID BOX

This little box can either be used as a box or as a decoration. The size is variable. Start by drawing a line and draw a semicircle on this line. Place the compass point, with the same radius, at one end of the semicircle and mark the centre and the point it crosses on the curve. Repeat from the other end. With the same radius setting, draw another semicircle so that it joins the first. Put the compass point on the join and mark the point it crosses on ths curve. Join all the marks, and four equilateral triangles will emerge. Add one glue flap to the base of the first triangle, two tucking flaps with slits, and two tabs to correspond with the slits, see diagram. Cut out the basic shape and score all the other lines. Stick the glue flap and place the gift inside and close the box tightly with the tabs – it is quite tricky to tuck in the tabs but ensures a very secure closure.

Above Basic plan for the pyramid box.

Right You can make your pyramid box to any size. Use plain or foiled light card, or decorate using the techniques described in the Decorating Chapter.

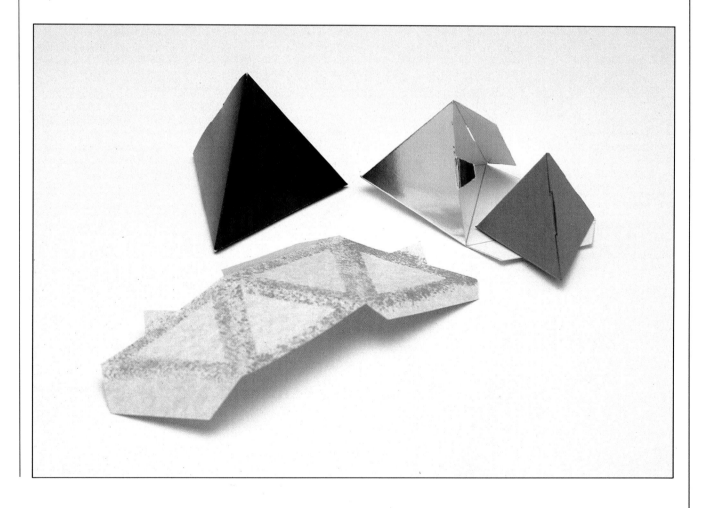

HEXAGONAL BOX

This box looks most impressive and is not as complicated as it appears. Once the size of the hexagon has been worked out it is quite easy to construct. If the box is being used for a circular gift this must fit *within* the hexagon and this should be worked out using scrap paper.

Draw a circle larger than the gift. Draw a horizontal line through the middle of the circle. Using the same radius setting, place the compass point on one of the intersections and mark the point it crosses on the curve. Move the compass to this point and repeat until you have six points around the circumference. Join these points and check whether the gift will fit into this hexagon – if not try again. Once this is correct, draw a plan following the diagram. The sides of the box are equal to the height of the gift and one side of the hexagon in length. The three flaps, top and bottom, are half the height of the hexagon. Cut out, score and fold. Check the angles of the flaps before glueing, in case any adjustments need to be made. Stick the glue flap and assemble the box. If necessary, stick down the tucking flaps on the base so that the box does not fall apart if the gift is heavy.

Above This hexagonal box has been made using embossed foil card. Filled with chocolates it makes an inexpensive yet impressive gift.

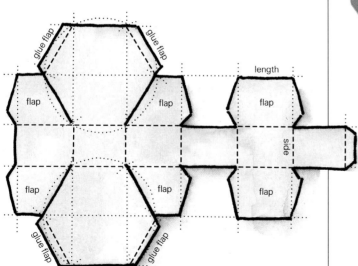

Above The basic plan for the hexagonal box.

PAPER SHOPPING BAGS

These bags are easy to make and can look extremely decorative. They can be made in many different sizes – tall and thin for bottles, short and wide for cosmetic items – and from many different types of paper. Matching gift tags, see page 74, can be added. Unusual handles can be made from toning or contrasting materials, such as plaited wool or ribbons.

Once you have mastered the basic method many variations are possible. Bags can be made in any size using normal gift-wrapping, but the larger the bag the thicker the paper will need to be. It is also possible to use plain paper and decorate it before assembly, see pages 32–50.

There are a few basic rules: all angles should be right angles (90°) so that the bag stands square when finished; the bottom flaps should be about ½ in (1 cm) less than the width of the sides; score the fold lines to give a crisper crease; this is essential on thicker paper and card.

Below For the handles, punch holes in the top edge and thread ribbons, cord or braid through them. The holes can act as closures or can be simply decorative.

BASIC BAG

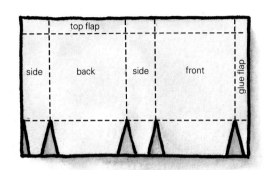

1 It is easiest to work on the wrong side of the paper. Decide on the size of the bag and draw the plan. Cut out the shape, removing the shaded areas. Score the dotted lines lightly, and fold and then unfold them.

3 Finally, glue the bottom flaps to each other – the side flaps to the back flap and the front flap on top of the side flaps.

2 Glue down the top flap, which adds strength and looks neater. Next glue the front flap to the side.

STRONG PAPER BAG

Making a bag which will carry a bottle or a heavy or large gift poses a few problems, but these can easily be overcome.

If a bottle or heavy gift is to be placed in the bag, it is advisable to glue a piece of card inside the base of the bag. To strengthen the top of the bag, add an extra strip of paper under the top flap. The basic plan is the same as for the ordinary bag, opposite, except that the measurements for all the sides will be identical and should be the diameter of the bottle plus ¼ in (6 mm). The height of the bag should be 2½ in (6 cm) more than the height of the bottle – so that the top edges can be drawn together.

When making a large bag it is quite simple to add a strong handle. Cut a piece of plain lightweight card the width of the bag and at least 3 in (7.5 cm) deep. Cut the hand shape out of the centre of the card and mark this hole on the bag plan. Cut these holes out of the paper on the bag and top flap, and glue the card stiffener in position. Continue as for the basic bag.

It is possible to fold the bag flat by scoring lines in addition to the ones on the basic plan. Practise with some scrap paper – this is not as complicated as it looks.

HEART-SHAPED BAG

The decorative heart-shaped bag shown on this page is deceptively simple. The design is based on a semicircle and can be made from many different types of paper or card. It is easy to alter the size by following the directions.

1 Draw a semicircle and mark a point about 65° from one edge, at C.

2 Mark another point 20° from C, then another at 65° and another at 20°. Join all these points at the centre.

3 Now divide both of the largest arcs in half, either by measuring or using a protractor. Draw semicircles on each half.

4 Cut out the whole shape and score all lines from the centre out to the edge and fold. Glue the shaded area to the heart shape.

Left Punch holes in the side panels and make handles. Decorate the bag if you wish. For inspiration see pages 32–50.

WRAPPING IDEAS

The art of wrapping and the art of giving could be said to be one and the same. A beautifully wrapped box shows that you have chosen and wrapped a gift with care.

The ideas in this chapter offer a basic introduction to the art of wrapping. The secret is to choose your wrapping papers with care, then to fold them neatly. Accessories such as ribbons, bows or gift tags are important decorative features which help to personalize a gift, but will not disguise a badly wrapped box. Almost any paper can be used to wrap a gift. Con-

ventional, patterned, gift-wrap papers are good, but consider using more unusual papers such as tissue paper, Ingres (Strathmore) paper and other papers from artists' supply stores and stationers. In particular, consider using decorated papers, see pages 32–50. A hand-decorated wrapping paper will give your gift that special personal touch. Some decorating techniques, such as folding and dipping, see pages 42–4, are best done with paper that is too thin to use as wrapping, so back them with another sheet for extra strength.

THE PERFECT WRAP

This is the best way to wrap a box so that it looks neat and well folded.
The method will work for a box of any shape.

1 Place the gift box on the wrapping paper. Trim the long edges of the sheet so that the overlap at the sides is the same as the height of the box. Fold over a hem of 1 in (2.5 cm) along one short edge.

2 Fix a strip of double-sided adhesive tape to the hem, almost the length of the box. Peel off the backing then stick the hem to the top of the box 2 in (5 cm) beyond the nearside edge.

3 Trim the other short side of the wrapping paper to length, so that when a 1 in (2.5 cm) hem is folded over and a strip of double-sided adhesive tape put on, the edge will fold up and stick to the box, level with the furthest edge.

4 Push in the sheet as shown. Be careful to keep it neat.

5 Fold in side triangles to lie flat against the box, forming a tapered point at the bottom.

6 Fix a small piece of double-sided adhesive tape to the tapered point at the bottom and fold up.

7 The box complete. Reinforce all the creases as the finishing touch.

PLEATED WRAPS

Here are three simple ways to pleat a sheet of wrapping paper to hold a name tag, a sheet of complementary wrapping paper or a decorative form. As ever, be careful to fold as neatly as possible, perhaps practising on scrap paper first.

3c Wrap as before to create a band of pleats set at an angle to the sides of the box.

1a For each, first make your item to be inserted between the pleats, preferably from thick paper or card. It can be any size, but the larger it is the farther apart the pleats will be. Place the card in the middle of the wrapping paper.

1b Carefully construct two pleats across the top and bottom of the inserted card so that the top pleat folds downwards and the bottom one folds upwards, trapping it between the pleats. The depth of the pleats should be at least ¾ in (2 cm).

2a Here the pleats run along the length of the wrap, so that in the finished wrap they lie across the box.

3a An unusual variation. Lay the card at an angle in the middle of the wrapping paper and form the pleats as before.

TIPS

Try experimenting with other patterns of pleats to create practical or decorative features on a gift-wrapped box: horizontal pleats crossing vertical pleats; pleats across a corner; lines of parallel pleats and so on. The effects can be surprisingly creative.

1c Continue to wrap as described in "The Perfect Wrap" above. This will create a wrapped gift with pleats running down the length of the box.

2b Construct the pleats and fold over the card as before.

3b Fold the excess paper behind (or cut it off), to restore the rectangular shape of the sheet.

2c Complete the wrap.

RIBBONS AND BOWS

RIBBONS

Ribbons are excellent ways to turn a plainly wrapped box into an attractively wrapped gift. Not all gift boxes need ribbons though – those that are wrapped in elaborately patterned gift-wrap paper may well be attractive enough as they are, or perhaps with an additional bow or gift tag.

Long lengths of gift-wrap ribbon can be purchased in many gift shops or stationers. Exciting and unconventional ribbons can be found in the fabric departments of stores. These range from hair ribbons to lace edging. Homemade ribbons can be made using strips cut from large sheets of paper decorated using the techniques described on pages 32–50. Alternatively, plaited wools make pretty ribbons.

An interesting use of ribbon is to plait or weave together two or more colours. The "under-and-over" pattern can vary and the ribbons can either be set square onto the box or set at an angle. See below for further ideas. Be careful not to cover too much of the gift with ribbons, or it may look over-decorated.

BOWS

Intricate bows already made up can often be purchased from gift shops or stationers, particularly in the weeks before Christmas. They are awkward to make well at home, requiring the construction of wooden templates and a lot of practice.

Here, though, is a simple but very attractive bow, sometimes called "My Lady". It works equally well made from gift-wrap ribbon, fabric ribbon or paper strips.

1 Cut a length of ribbon about 22 in (56 cm) long and twist it as shown, being careful to make both loops the same size. Secure the centre with a staple.

2 Cut another length of ribbon about 13 in (33 cm) long and form three loops as shown, beginning with the middle one. Trim off any excess. Check that it will fit between the loops of the other piece of ribbon.

3 Staple the second piece of ribbon to the first, being careful to line up all the layers and to centralize the second piece on top. To complete the bow, cut a V-shaped notch into the ends of the ribbon.

QUILLS

EQUIPMENT

1 Strips of paper
2 Glue
3 Cocktail sticks, matchsticks or dowel rod
4 Scissors – optional
5 Tweezers – optional
6 Waxed paper

BASIC COILS

Loose open coil.

Loose coil with the end stuck down. Most shapes are made from the loose coil.

Tight coil – the end is glued before removing from the stick.

Quilling uses rolled strips of paper to form shapes, which can be glued together to make patterns. The designs can then be used in numerous ways, for example, glued on cards for gift tags or greetings cards, as decorations for boxes, as mobiles or stencils. Quilling is sometimes known as paper filigree and was used by monks in the 15th century to make panels of imitation gold filigree. In the Victorian period quilling was considered a very lady-like pursuit and tea-caddies were a popular item for decoration.

Traditionally the strips are ⅛ in (3 mm) wide and the length can vary. The strips can sometimes be bought in stationery shops or can be laboriously cut by hand, or carnival streamers can be used – these are usually a little wider, but the principle remains the same.

Using a cocktail stick, matchstick or thin dowel rod with a split, place one end of the strip in the split and turn it slowly and evenly so that the strip remains level. When the paper is completely rolled, squeeze it lightly to make a tight curve before removing the stick. This coil is a loose open coil.

Pear drop – squeeze the side that has been stuck, to a point.

Petal – as pear drop but curved gently at the same time as squeezing to form the point.

Eye-shape – both ends are pointed and the whole shape is elongated slightly.

Leaf-shape – as eye-shape but curved gently in both directions.

S-shape – rolled in opposite directions from both ends.

Scroll-shape – rolled in the same direction from both ends.

V-shape – creased at the halfway point and rolled outwards.

Heart-shape – as V-shape but rolled inwards.

Triangle – squeezed in three places.

DECORATING WITH QUILLS

Patterns can be planned in advance or built up as you go along. In either case, it is best to work on a piece of waxed paper so that the design can be moved around as the work progresses, without getting stuck. This is especially important if the piece is to be used on its own. If the design is being made as a decoration for an object, it can be worked directly onto the object by glueing the centre of the shape and placing each part carefully in position. Tweezers or an extra cocktail stick will be useful. Finished designs can be sprayed with paint or varnish.

GIFT TAGS

Gift tags are one of the finishing touches of a present and a little imagination can make even this small piece of paper quite special. They can be quick and easy to make or quite intricate.

Gift tags can be single or double. They can be attached with a punched hole and cord or stuck directly onto the parcel. There are many types of cord available in the shops with which to attach the tag – plait together threads that tone with the colours from the paper design; ribbons; wool or metallic string.

Use card cut to the required size or shape, scored and folded, if making a double card. If you use paper, it may be necessary to glue this to another piece of paper so that it is not too floppy. This method could also be used to make a card from the paper used to wrap the gift.

Plain tags can be decorated with stickers, quilled shapes (see below) and miniature origami.

TWIST-OUTS, CUT-AWAYS AND POP-UPS

These three similar techniques are exciting ways to create imaginative three-dimensional greetings cards or decorations. They are all simple to make, but will be best understood if you first follow the instructions that explain how to produce a basic example of each technique.

TWIST-OUTS

Twist-outs are particularly ingenious ways to create three-dimensional cards, suspended decorations or simply beautiful shapes to be admired. Use thin card for finished examples – paper is too weak and thick card too cumbersome to bend easily.

EQUIPMENT

1 Card
2 A scalpel or craft knife
3 Something to cut on
4 A pair of scissors
5 A pencil and a ruler

Below right This technique, once mastered, will produce decorations and sculptural forms of great beauty. Study the examples in the photograph, then experiment with your own ideas.

1 For the basic method, draw line AB down the centre of a piece of scrap card or paper.

2 With a blade, incise line C to D, so that the incision starts and ends on AB. (Note that AC is shorter than DB.)

3 Next, incise line E to F, so that the incision once again starts and ends on AB. Note that E is below C and F is below D.

4 Pull edge GH towards you and push IJ away from you, forming short creases between CE and DF.

5 The centre of the card will twist out from its frame.

VARIATIONS

The following are variations of the basic technique. The principle is that line AB can be anywhere on a sheet of card. The incisions can be any shape, but they must begin and end on AB, so that CE and DF can be creased along one uninterrupted line.

Draw AB along a diagonal, so that when incisions are made, the centre twists out from its frame along a diagonal axis.

Draw AB towards the lefthand edge, so that the centre twists out a long way on the right but very little on the left.

Draw AB in an arbitrary position and doodle incisions on it at random.

G R E E T I N G S   C A R D S

Here are three twist-outs in the form of greetings cards. The letters could be re-worked to say HAPPY BIRTHDAY, GET WELL, GOOD LUCK, etc. Other good festive themes include candles, stars, baubles or stockings.

If you draw AB on the horizontal, this creates possibilities for sculptural cards on a wide variety of themes, including all those suggested above. Remember, any shape – no matter how unlikely – can be made to twist out. Invent your own to suit an occasion which requires you to send a card.

Right Twist-outs make highly individual greetings cards. The wordings and figurations can be altered to suit every occasion.

Once you have understood and practised the basic twist-out technique, try making concentric incisions.

The simplest way of doing this is to retain AB as the single line along which all incisions start and end. Cut all the incisions, then twist out each alternate frame, working towards the centre.

An intriguing elaboration is to introduce a second line (A_1B_1) on which to start and end incisions. Whereas the previous design creates vertical frames, this will also produce horizontal ones. Other lines (A_2B_2, A_3B_3 etc.) may be introduced to make concentric shapes twist out at many different angles.

Right Concentric twist-outs make fascinating mobiles. Simply thread a strong piece of thread through the middle of the outer frame.

CUT-AWAYS

This easy technique is an interesting way to make a shape of card project beyond a crease, creating an unusual silhouette. It looks particularly good when used on a greetings card. Use card of thin to medium thickness.

1 Draw line AB down the middle.

2 With a blade, incise line C to D starting and ending on AB.

3 Make a mountain crease between AC and DB, so that corner F bends backwards to touch E. Do not crease between C and D.

4 The card should look like this, with a rectangle of card projecting beyond the crease.

VARIATIONS

You could make a cut-away nose and pipe, with the outline of the other half of the card cut to the profile of a head.

When the top half of the numerals are made to project beyond the crease, the card beyond the bottom half of the numerals can be cut away to complete their silhouettes.

Here the card beyond the heart has been lost to one side of crease AB.

POP-UPS

Of the three techniques explained in this chapter, pop-ups can become the most technical. This section shows how versatile the simpler pop-up techniques are. If you wish to see more complex examples, look at some of the remarkably clever pop-up books in the children's section of a good bookshop. Pop-ups can be used in combination with the cut-away techniques explained in the previous section, helping to break the symmetry of a pop-up shape. Use thin card, but practise on stiff paper.

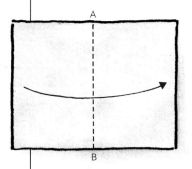

BASIC METHOD
1 Crease a piece of card along AB and fold the card in half along the crease.

2 With a pair of scissors, make two cuts from crease AB almost half-way across the sheet.

3 Fold the section between the cuts over to the right, pulling it over as far as it will go, connecting the ends of the cuts with a crease.

4 Unfold the centre section.

5 Open the sheet.

6 Don't flatten the sheet, but keep a valley crease along AB.

7 Lift up the thin belt of card between the cuts, so that the valley crease down the middle of the belt pops up and becomes a mountain crease.

VARIATIONS A The cuts do not have to be perpendicular to crease AB, as step 2. They can be angled as shown here.

B The crease made in step 3 need not be parallel to AB – it can be at any angle. The cuts can also be any shape.

C To make a "second-generation pop-up", follow steps 1 to 7 of the basic method. Fold the pop-up flat and make two cuts only into the nearside crease (**top**), then proceed as in steps 2 to 7. The second generation pop-up complete (**above**). By repeating this process a third generation, then a fourth, etc, can be made to pop up.

Left Suggestions for pop-up cards are illustrated here. Some are first-generation pop-ups, some have two or more generations, and others have incorporated cut-away techniques.

MULTI POP-UPS

The pop-ups made so far have all been built up from a central crease AB (see step 1). However, by starting with more than one crease, you can make decorations which are fully three-dimensional. Here is one suggestion.

1 Cut out a piece of thin card four times as long as it is high, with a small tab on the end for glueing. Pleat it into eighths, alternating the mountain and valley creases.

2 Make 24 cuts as shown.

3 Pleat the strip and glue the tab to hold the pleats in the shape of a cross. Pull out the belts of card between the cuts.

Right The cross-shape opened out, with suggested variations.

STATIONERY

CARD FOLDS AND IDEAS

Fig 1

CARD FOLDS AND IDEAS

There are many ways to fold a piece of card or paper to form the basis of a greetings card. Some are simple and well known, whereas others are a little more complicated. The illustrations here show some basic starting points and the photographs indicate how they can be made into attractive greetings cards. Use thin card, except for Figs 2, 6 and 7, for which thicker paper is best. See page 8 for a guide to paper and card weights.

The techniques shown in other chapters of the book can be adapted to form cards, especially those in Decorating Paper (pages 32–50), Origami (pages 106–173) and Twist-outs, Cut-aways and Pop-ups (pages 76–82). Think of the type of card fold and paper technique that best suit the occasion – the variations are endless.

Left These cards are all made from the basic folds shown above: 1 and 2 are designs cut from a single fold (see Fig 1); 3 is a single fold with a cut-out shape glued on; 4 is a double fold (see Fig 2) with a paper weaving decoration attached to the face; 5 is a single fold decorated with a collage made of adhesive-backed paper; 6 is a single fold card with a basic envelope, see page 86.

ADDITIONAL FOLDS

Fig 3

Fig 4

Fig 5

Fig 6

Fig 7

Left Most of these cards are made from folds shown above: 1 is made from the fold in Fig 6; 2 is made from the fold shown in Fig 7 and decorated with purchased stickers; 3 is made from the fold in Fig 4 – the righthand flap has been cut out to act as a mount for the photograph; 4 and 5 are made from the fold in Fig 5 and are both cut-outs; 6 is made from the fold in Fig 2 using the pop-up technique explained on page 82.

BASIC ENVELOPE

Having practised some of the techniques in the previous chapters, it will no longer be necessary for you to buy greetings cards or even an envelope to fit any card, because you will be able to make your own. It is also easy to decorate stationery and to make a holder as a really unusual gift.

1 Measure the card and add ¼ in (½ cm) to the length and the width (**top**). If the card is an irregular shape (**above**) add extra to the widest points.

2 Plan the size of paper required for the envelope: the side flaps should be at least 1 in (2.5 cm); the bottom flap should be three-quarters the width of the card plus ½ in (1 cm) for closing; and the top flap should be a quarter the width plus ½ in (1 cm).

3 Draw this shape on your chosen paper and cut it out. (Use a coin to draw the curves of the side flaps.) Taper the top and bottom flaps. Score the dotted lines.

4 Turn in the side flaps. Apply glue to the side edges of the bottom flap, turn it up and stick it to the side flaps. The envelope is now ready to be used. To close the envelope, either use glue or double-sided adhesive tape along the top flap.

Right You could line the basic envelope using plain coloured tissue paper or folded and dyed paper, see pages 42–5. Add the lining before you turn in the side flaps. Cut a piece of lining paper the width of the envelope and the length of the envelope minus the bottom flap. Glue it in position before assembling the envelope.

FOLDED ENVELOPE 1

1 Begin with a square of paper, creased vertically down the middle. Fold the bottom edge up to the top and press it flat in the middle to find the mid-point of the square.

2 Fold the bottom edge up to the centre.

3 Fold in the sides, as shown.

4 Fold the loose corners behind at the bottom.

5 Fold the top corners into the centre vertical crease.

6 Crease across the base of the top triangles, tucking them inside the pocket. This locks the envelope shut.

7 The complete envelope. Write the address on the side without any folds.

Left The envelopes in the photograph have been folded from a piece of paper the same size as the pieces on which they are lying.

FOLDED ENVELOPE 2

1 Using a square piece of paper, crease a diagonal line BD and unfold it. Fold corners A and C onto the crease, so that the new creases made do not quite run down to corner D.

2 Crease and unfold G to H.

3 Fold up D so that corner G lies on edge EA and corner H on CF.

4 Fold D inside, tucking it behind A and C; this locks G and H flat. Fold in E and F, butting them hard against the edges that run up to G and H.

5 Slide B under edge GH and push it until it will not go any further. Flatten and crease.

6 The complete envelope. To unlock it, pull out corner B.

Left Again, the envelopes in the photograph have been folded from a piece of paper the same size as the pieces on which they are lying.

STATIONERY HOLDER

EQUIPMENT

1 Board $\frac{1}{16}$ in (1.5 mm) thick
2 Covering and lining material
3 Book cloth (see below)
4 Pencil, ruler, compass or dividers
5 Knife and scissors
6 Glue
7 Bone folder
8 Newsprint or computer paper for scrap paper

2 To cut cloth for the corners use a scrap of paper along the marked line and add $\frac{1}{2}$ in (1 cm) to overlap the edges, see Fig 1. Measure the square edges and cut two squares of book cloth. Cut across them diagonally to make triangles to cover the corners.

This design can be made to take most sizes of writing paper and notecards.

Measure the stationery and add $\frac{3}{4}$ in (2 cm) to the length and the width; these two measurements will determine the size of the boards. Cut two boards to size, making sure that the corners are square and that the grain runs from top to bottom, see page 9. To allow for turn-ins, covering materials should overlap all edges by $\frac{1}{2}$ in (1 cm), unless otherwise stated. Lining materials should be $\frac{1}{2}$ in (12 mm) smaller than the overall measurements of the board. Draw a line down one side of the board one-fifth of the overall width. Mark this with a pair of compasses or dividers and also mark the corner on the diagonal. Repeat for the other board. (See Fig 1.)

1 Cut the bookcloth to size – twice as wide as the marked line plus at least $\frac{3}{4}$ in (2 cm) to accommodate the contents, and as long as the boards plus turn-ins. Cut a lining piece – remember constants.

⅕ of cover width   ⅕ of cover width

Fig 1

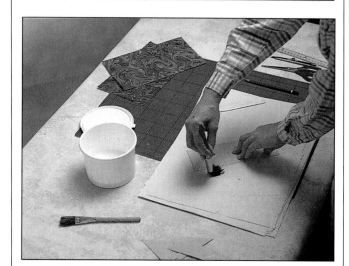

3 Brush glue onto the wrong side of the book-cloth cut for the spine – the glue should be the consistency of thick cream. Using a firm brush and scrap paper, work the glue from the centre of the piece out towards and over the edges onto the scrap.

4 Position the spine on the boards between the marked lines and turnover the edges using a bone folder or clean fingers.

5 Glue the lining strip in position and, using the bone folder, press the bookcloth well to form a groove; start from one side and work across.

6 Mark the position of the triangular piece and trim off the corner.

7 Glue the piece into position on the diagonal line and press it towards the corner. Turn over and, using the bone folder, press the edge down and work the mitre neatly into boards. Finally bring the second edge over and press it down. Repeat for the other three corners.

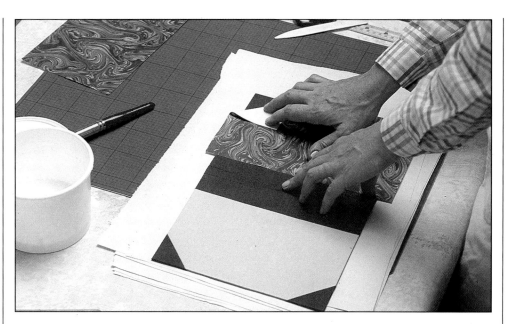

8 Now, mark the covering material, remembering to add extra for the turn-ins on the edges and slightly overlapping the book cloth at the spine. Position the covering material on the board and, holding it down firmly, fold back one corner so that it just covers the book cloth triangle, and crease. Repeat for the other corner. Remove from the board and trim away the corners at the folded crease.

9 Before gluing mark the position on the wrong side.

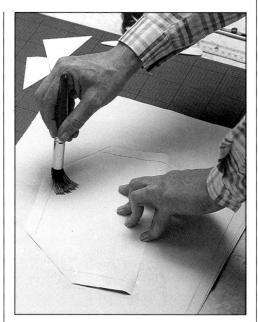

10 Work quickly, because the covering material may curl when moistened with glue.

11 Place the glued piece on the board and cover it with a piece of scrap paper. Smooth it over gently with the bone folder to remove any air bubbles. The scrap paper protects the covering material from becoming shiny with rubbing.

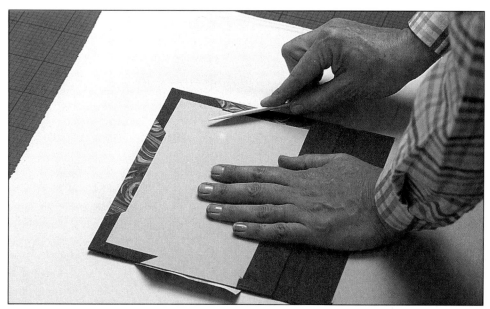

12 Now turn in the edges neatly, adding more glue if necessary.

13 If you want ribbon ties attach them at this stage. Cut two lengths of about 12 in (30 cm). Using a knife or chisel, cut a hole the width of the ribbon in the centre of both boards ½ in (1 cm) from the side edge.

14 Push the ribbons through these holes and glue them in place. Cover the right side with a scrap of board and hammer it to close and flatten the incision (this step is not essential).

LINING

To line the folder there is a variety of possibilities: you could line the righthand board with plain paper with flaps to protect the contents of the holder and to stop them falling out; you could line the lefthand board quite simply with a piece of plain paper glued in place or it could have a pocket attached for envelopes; the pocket could be made of decorative paper or a different shape – see the photograph of the finished project.

For the righthand lining, cut a piece of paper 1½ times as wide and 1½ times as long as the boards, with the grain running from top to bottom, see Fig 2. For the lefthand lining, cut one piece the same size as the boards, less the constants for lining. For the pocket, cut one piece half the length of the boards and the full width plus 1 in (2.5 cm).

ALTERNATIVES

If bookcloth is not available, it is possible to make your own by laminating cloth material to paper. Brush a thin layer of glue onto lightweight paper and smooth the paper carefully onto the cloth. Cover it with scrap paper and smooth it gently all over with a bone folder or the side of your hand to remove the air bubbles. Allow it to dry under weights – a pile of books or something similar.

1 Position the lefthand lining on the righthand lining paper so that the lefthand edges are together and the excess equal at top and bottom. Using the lefthand lining as a guide, score the righthand lining paper right across the top and bottom and down the side. Trim away the top and bottom righthand rectangles. Score a second line ¼ in (6 mm) from the previous scores towards the outside edge of all three flaps. Crease and fold-in – the paper now appears the same size as the board minus the lining constants, and is ready to glue into position.

2 Score the paper cut for the pocket, using a ruler and a bone folder, ½ in (1 cm) in from the top and bottom edges. Fold and glue down one edge. This is to strengthen the top edge of the pocket. Place the pocket on the lefthand lining paper so that it overlaps equally at both sides. Score and fold in these edges.

score and fold   cut away

score and fold

score and fold   cut away

Fig 2

3 Trim away the double fold of the pocket as a mitre to reduce bulk. Taper, very slightly, the lower side edges of the lining for the same reason.

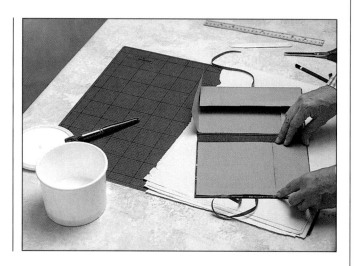

4 Glue the folded flaps of the pocket to the lining paper. Then glue the whole piece into position on the lefthand board.

TABLE DECORATIONS

SERVIETTE FOLDS

The use of paper as a means of table decoration is often forgotten. Most people take paper and its uses for granted and, although paper serviettes are used each day, it is seldom that one thinks of folding them decoratively or of using a little imagination to make simple place name cards or serviette rings. Using the ideas found in this chapter, it is easy to draw to-gether the whole table setting. Make a theme for the whole setting by choosing a colour, perhaps picked out from the dinner service or table cloth, or use a topic to suit the season.

SAIL SERVIETTE

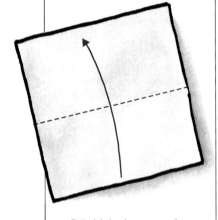

1 Fold the bottom edge up to the top.

2 Fold down the top righthand corner.

3 Fold the bottom right corner across to the left edge.

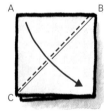

4 Fold corner A downwards. Note B and C.

5 Open corner C, flattening the crease BC.

6 Fold up the tip of corner C . . .

7 . . . to lock and complete the sail serviette.

Above This is a simple, attractive serviette, quick to make and easy to unfold.

FLAME SERVIETTE

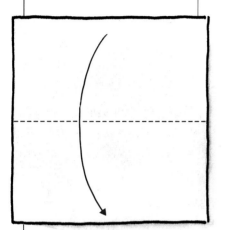

1 Fold the top edge down to the bottom.

2 Fold the righthand edge over to the left.

Left This fold is more complex than the previous one, but makes a spectacular display. Fold two together of different colours for extra visual effect.

7 Hold the serviette firmly at the bottom. There are five layers of corners at the top. Tug corner C as shown, pulling it as far out as possible. Do the same with corner D next to it, but not pulling it as far. Repeat on the other side, pulling B further than A.

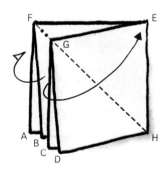

3 Look carefully at the lettered corners. Fold A and B behind to touch E and fold C and D to the front to also touch E. Crease FH and GH . . .

4 . . . like this.

5 Pleat the triangle into six equal divisions, to look . . .

6 . . . like this.

8 The flame serviette is complete. To hold its shape, the design needs to be placed in a wine glass or tumbler.

PLACE NAME CARDS

1 Lightweight to medium-weight card
2 Card for templates
3 Paper for decorations (foil, crêpe, etc.)
4 A cocktail stick or straw
5 Glue and adhesive tape
6 Pencil and ruler
7 Knife or a pair of scissors

As with other items in this chapter, the place name cards can be quite plain or very decorative. Folding ones, which stand up on the table, look more professional and are usually easier to read.

The names can be written with a coloured pen or silver or gold markers as well as ordinary ink. The size of the card can vary a little depending on your handwriting and the length of the name, but 3–3½ in (7.5–8.5 cm) by 1¼–1½ in (3–4 cm) should allow sufficient room.

Above Here a simple name card is illustrated.

Above If one side is cut shorter than the other, the angle of the card on the table will be flatter. Draw, cut and score these cards. Then decorate them with stickers, stencil patterns, etc. Write the name on the card before folding and placing it in position.

Above This place name card is an adaptation of the basic card.

Right The extension could have other shapes glued to it to suit another season. It could also have quilled shapes, see page 73, glued to it or a miniature origami design.

1 For a Christmas tree design you will need four of these shapes; cut them from any lightweight decorative paper. Fold each shape in half.

glue   glue

glue pairs together

2 Glue the folded halves to each other leaving two folded halves free.

glue to extension

3 Glue the two free folded halves (see inset) to the side extension of the name card.

1 For the name card part of this decoration, mark a piece of card (**left**). Cut out the card, score and fold it and then glue section D under section A.

2 To make the tree use very lightweight paper. Cut out the shaped piece and attach adhesive tape along the straight uncut edge (**right**). The slits should be ⅛ in (3 mm) apart.

3 Take a drinking straw and, holding it at an angle of 45°, roll the adhesive tape around the straw, starting from the narrow end. The slits will fall into a tree shape. Slip the straw through the hole in the top of the card, cut it to size and then, if necessary, secure it through the base with a pin so that the tree stands upright.

Right It is possible to wrap the shaped and slit piece around the straw at an angle of 30°. This will result in a less bushy tree with a wider shape (**near right**). If you prefer this shape, wrap the straw with a strip of paper before winding the shaped piece around because the increased angle means that the straw will not otherwise be covered. Also the initial piece can be reduced in length by at least 2 in (5 cm). You could attach a miniature carnation, see pages 100–1, to a drinking straw or cocktail stick and use it in the same way. Cut leaves from suitable paper and attach them to the stem, which could be covered with stem tape or painted green.

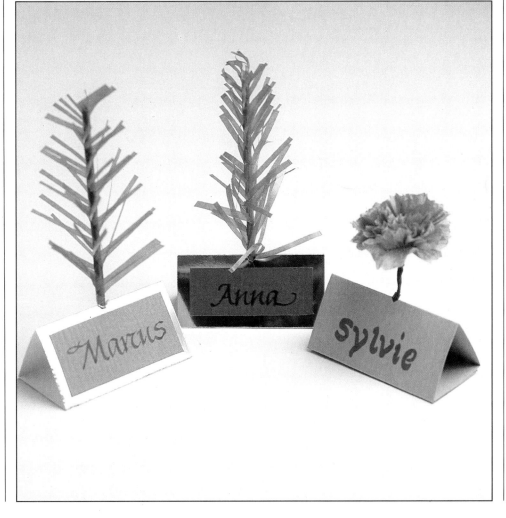

PAPER FLOWERS

1 Stub wire (often coated with green plastic), available from florists and good craft shops
2 Stem tape, also available from florists
3 Crêpe paper – good-quality crêpe paper has plenty of stretch
4 Pinking shears, if available.

Paper flowers are fun to make and can look quite realistic, even though they should not pretend to take the place of real flowers. As the leaves are difficult to make, it is a good idea to use real greenery in the vase; this will also help to hold the rather spindly wire stems of the paper flowers.

CARNATIONS

1 The crêpe paper should be folded to a width of 5 in (12.5 cm). Cutting through all the thicknesses with the pinking shears, cut off the straight edge and then a piece 3½ in (9 cm) long. Do not unfold the paper but cut off the sides to make several rectangles with pinked edges.

2 Four layers make an average carnation, two layers make a small one and one layer makes a bud, which should be trimmed to shape on completion. Hold the layers widthways and stretch them evenly, being careful not to use your thumb tips as this will make a cupped curve at the centre.

3 Turn the paper so that the short edge is facing up. Accordion pleat the length of the stretched piece – about five to six pleats ½ in (1 cm) wide can be fitted into the piece. It is important that the cut edges face upwards at the beginning and the end. Place a stub wire in the centre at the front of the pleated paper with about 1½ in (4 cm) showing above the folds.

4 Fold the wire down behind and twist it to secure it. Fan out the pleats to check that both sides are even.

5 Now separate the layers, starting with the innermost layer, which must be pulled up as close to the wire as possible. Continue in this way until all the layers are pulled up.

6 To make the calyx, take a piece of crêpe paper and fold it loosely into a narrow strip. Wrap it around the base of the flower, twisting the paper as it is wrapped to make it slightly triangular in shape. If you wish, use a touch of glue to secure it.

7 Take the stem tape, give it a good pull to stretch it, and then wrap it firmly around the calyx, holding the wire and pulling it downwards, while twisting. It sounds complicated, but a little practice will make it clear. If stem tape is not available, a strip of green crêpe paper ½ in (1 cm) wide can be used and secured with glue at the top and bottom. Add leaves if you wish.

Left Make your carnations of various sizes and use different-coloured crêpe paper for a lovely display. If the flowers become crushed, they can be revived by holding them over steam and fluffing them up.

ROSES

Fig 1

Fig 2

Left Petal template –
see step 1.

Above Sepal template
– see step 6.

EQUIPMENT

1 Stub wire (available as
for carnations)
2 Stem tape (available as
for carnations)
3 Florist's wire
4 Double-sided crêpe
paper
5 Pencil
6 A pair of scissors
7 Blunt knife

1 Place the petal
template (see Fig 1) on
the double-sided crêpe
paper and fold it over so
that there are nine petals,
or measure a strip
approximately 18½ in
(47 cm) and pleat it. Cut
out the petal shape,
making sure that the sides
remain joined. Unfold and
cut off three petals.

2 Decide which colour
should be on the outside
of the petals and work with
the other colour facing you.
Using a blunt knife or the
back of the scissors, curl
the petal tops by placing
the blade behind the petal
and gently but firmly
drawing the crêpe paper
over the blade.

3 Having curled all the
petal tops, cup them in
the centre by stretching
each petal widthways with
your thumbs.

5 Now roll the first petal tightly around the wire. Ease the remaining five petals gently into shape – closed or open – and secure them by wrapping them with florist's wire. Twist the ends and bend them down.

4 Take a stub wire and thread it through the petals at one end and turn it over to secure.

6 Take the three separated petals and arrange them around the outside and secure them as before. The final three petals can be omitted to give a smaller rose, and if the petals are formed more tightly the result will be more bud-like. Prepare the calyx as for the carnation. Add sepals if you wish (see Fig 2) and wrap the stem as for the carnation.

Right Again, use various colours of crêpe paper for a truly marvellous and realistic bouquet of flowers.

103

ORIGAMI

SYMBOLS

Symbols are the core of any book about origami. They need not all be learnt at once, but it is important to know at least the symbols for valley and mountain folds. When you see an unfamiliar symbol, refer back to this page to see what it means.

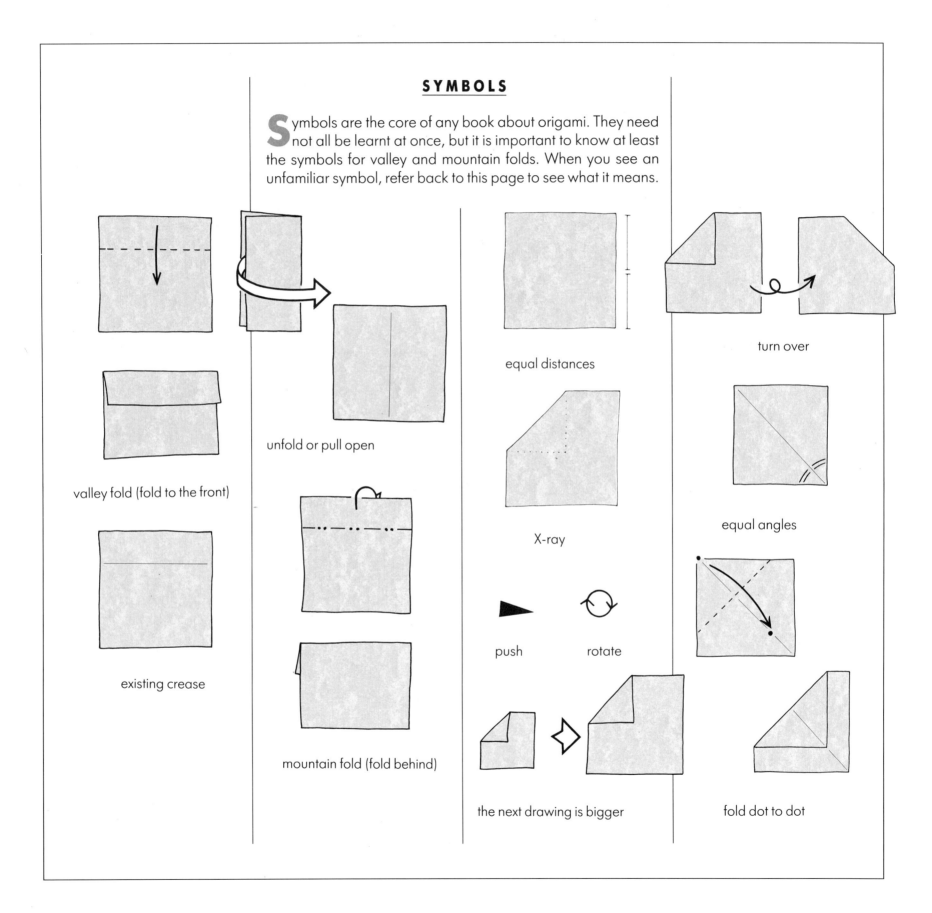

valley fold (fold to the front)

existing crease

unfold or pull open

mountain fold (fold behind)

equal distances

X-ray

push   rotate

the next drawing is bigger

turn over

equal angles

fold dot to dot

FIRST PRINCIPLES

HOW TO MAKE A SQUARE

Most bought papers are oblong and have to be trimmed square. There are several ways to do this, but here is the best.

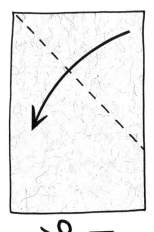

1 Fold a triangle. Turn over.

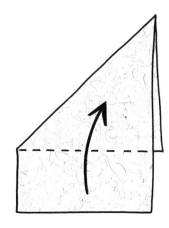

2 Fold up the oblong exactly level with the edge of the triangle behind.

3 Cut off the excess oblong of paper with a non-serrated kitchen knife which has a blade at least 5 in (12 cm) long.

4 Hold the paper firmly against a hard, level surface and cut along the crease with a series of smooth slicing movements.

5 The completed square. Done properly, the edge is pleasingly clean.

HOW TO MAKE A CREASE

This may seem pedantic to the eager beginner, but it is important to know how to make an accurate crease. Just one inaccuracy early in a sequence will throw all the later creases out of alignment, creating a clumsy design.

The basic rule is very simple. Keep rotating the paper (or turning it over), so that every crease is made from left to right across your body (or right to left, if preferred), and the part of the paper which folds over when the crease is made moves *away* from your body, not towards it or to one side.

■ When you see a crease on a diagram which does not run from left to right, *rotate the paper* so that it does, then make the crease.

■ When you see a mountain fold symbol, turn the paper over (or open up the inside), making a *valley* fold, then turn back over (or close up) again.

■ Creases are not chores to be done as quickly as possible on the way to completing a design. They should be enjoyed. Some experts believe that the pleasure of origami lies more in the making of creases and the manipulation of paper, than in achieving a completed design, or looking at one. Take time out to *enjoy* your folding.

1

1

1

2 A correct crease.

2 An incorrect crease.

2 An incorrect crease.

BASIC TECHNIQUES

The root of paper folding is the *valley fold* (and its opposite the *mountain fold*). Such basic creases need no explanation, but more complex techniques do. The most common technique is the *reverse fold* and its opposite the *outside reverse fold* (most things in origami it seems, have an opposite). They are explained below, as is another technique, the *squash fold*. Other techniques are explained with the designs.

If you are unfamiliar with the reverse and squash folds, please take a little time to fold the basic examples and studies which follow.

Studies

Here are further examples. Look at them carefully before attempting them.

1 Reverse

2

1 Reverse

2

REVERSE FOLD

Basic Example

1 Fold in half.

2 Fold the corner across to the right . . .

3 . . . then fold it around the back along the same crease.

4 Unfold.

5 Hold as shown. Swing the top corner down between the layers . . .

6 . . . like this. Flatten the creases. The reverse fold complete. The reverse fold described above is notated like this:

1

2 Reverse

If you are unfamiliar with the reverse fold, prepare by folding the crease backwards and forwards as in steps 2–4 of the basic example above.

OUTSIDE REVERSE FOLD

Basic Example

1 Fold the corner across to the left . . .

2 . . . then fold it around the back along the same crease.

3 Unfold.

4 Spread A and B.

5 Refold both short creases as valleys, lifting C.

6 Collapse back in half.

7 The outside reverse fold complete.

■ The outside reverse fold described above is notated like this:

1 Outside reverse

2

SQUASH FOLD

Basic Example

1 Fold in half.

2 Fold dot to dot.

3 Unfold, so that A stands upright.

4 Squash A flat, opening the pocket . . .

5 . . . like this. Flatten the paper. The squash fold complete.

1 Squash

2

TRADITIONAL DESIGNS

Traditional designs are designs of uncertain origin. Nobody knows where they were first folded, when, by whom and sometimes why. Some may be a thousand years old or more.

Curiously, almost all (surviving) traditional designs of note have variations, whereas most modern classic designs do not. The Junk and Sampan for example, can be folded in numerous ways, not just to achieve the same form, but to achieve simpler or more complex variations. Even the elementary Banger and Glider can be folded in several different ways. Perhaps this has helped them to survive: each generation can remember the *basis* of a design but forgets the detail and so has to re-invent it.

What qualities make the basis of a particular design so memorable? Eastern symbolism aside, perhaps it is because something about that design is unique: the Banger makes a loud noise, the Dish is circular, the Sampan turns completely inside-out and so on. What's more, they all have a clever or entertaining finish to make the folding worthwhile. Origami is very much a performing art.

Some knowledgeable paper-folders have little regard for traditional designs, preferring the fireworks of complex modern creations. However, like popular melodies, these designs have endured because of an appeal more profound than mere fashion. Their simplicity is deceptive, transcending cultures.

BANGER

This is one of the most entertaining of all paper folds and certainly the loudest! Practise Step 7, because good technique will increase the volume of the bang. Use a rectangle of thin or medium-weight paper, at least 10 × 15 in (25 × 37 cm). Larger sheets will produce louder noises.

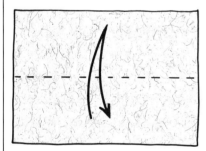

1 Fold one long edge across to the other. Crease and unfold.

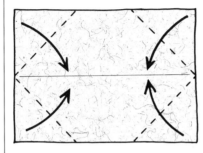

2 Fold in the corners to the centre crease.

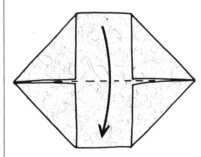

3 Fold in half along the Step 1 crease.

4 Mountain fold across the middle. Crease and unfold.

5 Check that the centre crease made in Step 1 is a mountain (if it's a valley, turn the paper over), then fold the sharp corners across to the right.

6 Mountain fold in half. Note the double corner at X.

7 Hold X as shown. Bend your elbow so that the Banger is behind your head, then whip it downwards very quickly. The paper will unfold with a loud **BANG**! If it doesn't, check that you haven't held the paper upside down and try to move your arm quicker.

CROWN

Hats are a popular origami subject. This design creates a large, well-locked hat from a relatively small sheet and because of its square shape it will grip your head well. Use a square of sturdy paper 15 × 15 in (37 × 37 cm) for a child and a little larger for an adult head.

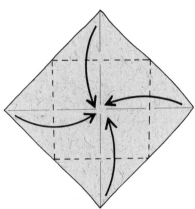

2 Fold the corners to the centre.

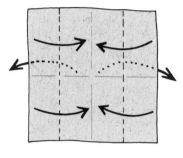

4 Fold the top and bottom edges to the centre crease, allowing corners A and B to flip out from behind . . .

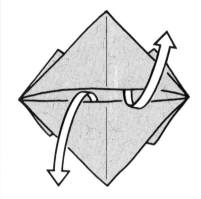

6 Pull open the slit . . .

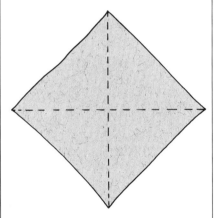

1 Crease and unfold both diagonals.

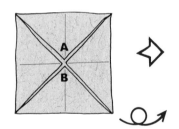

3 Note A and B. Turn over.

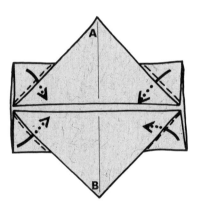

5 . . . like this. Fold the small triangles under the large ones.

7 . . . to complete the Crown. Press it into shape, squaring the sides.

B I R D

Whereas some origami designs can be naturalistic, other designs, such as this one, are really symbols. Here is a bird – not a duck or a swan – just a bird: it has a head, wings and a tail, so it *must* be one, even though it doesn't look like any particular species. Is the design a remarkable distillation of form, or merely an example of inadequate technique? Surely the former.

Use a 6–8 in (15–20 cm) square of paper.

1 Make a mountain crease along a diagonal. Unfold.

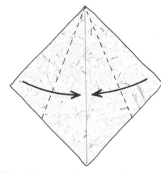

2 Fold two edges to the centre crease. Be careful to make a neat corner at the top.

3 Fold dot to dot.

4 Fold the sharp corner back up a little way. The exact distance is unimportant.

5 Mountain fold in half.

6 Lift the beak away from the neck. Squeeze flat the back of the head to make new creases.

7 Lift the neck away from the body. Squeeze flat the base of the neck to make new creases.

8 The Bird is complete.

CUP

Few origami designs are practical. Made from a waterproof material such as metallic kitchen foil or greaseproof paper, this simple design will hold a liquid without leaking through an open edge. Turned upside down, it will even make an excellent hat. Flap B can be brought down to form a visor. Use a 6–8 in (15–20 cm) square of paper.

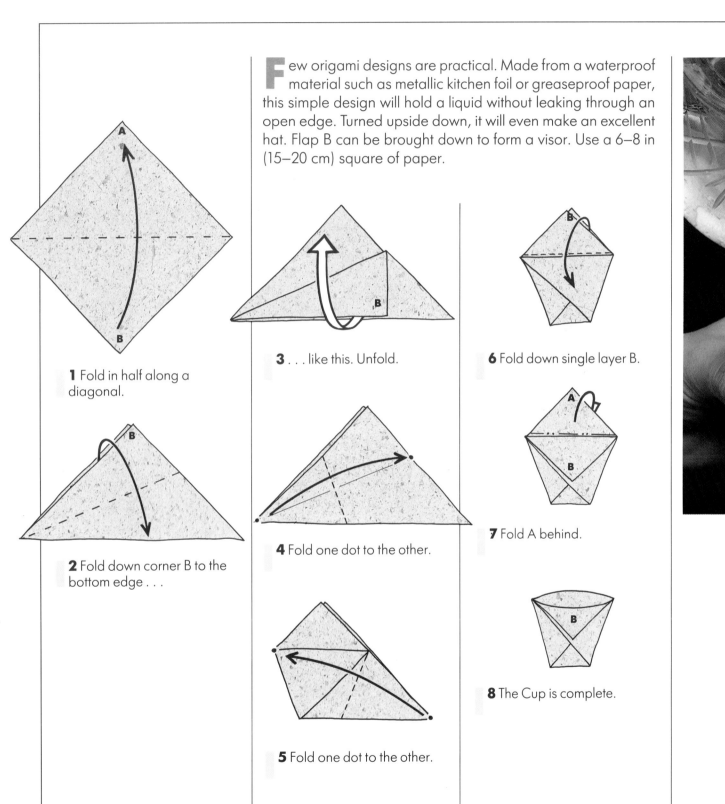

1 Fold in half along a diagonal.

2 Fold down corner B to the bottom edge . . .

3 . . . like this. Unfold.

4 Fold one dot to the other.

5 Fold one dot to the other.

6 Fold down single layer B.

7 Fold A behind.

8 The Cup is complete.

WATERLILY

This is the full version of a spectacular napkin fold sometimes seen in restaurants. Note the remarkable manner in which the uninteresting shape made up to Step 6 is gradually opened up and transformed into the beautiful completed design. Use a paper napkin. Ordinary paper will rip at Step 7.

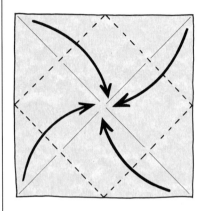

1 Fold the corners to the centre.

2 Again, fold the corners to the centre.

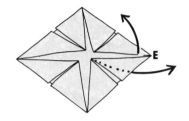

3 Once again, fold the corners to the centre.

4 Turn over. Note ABCD.

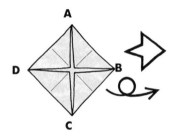

5 Yet again fold the corners to the centre.

6 Note E. Hold all the layers flat and pull out corner A mentioned in Step 4.

7 Hold as shown. Pull A forcibly upwards, so that it unpeels around E . . .

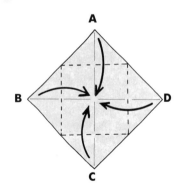

8 . . . like this. Repeat with B C and D, keeping hold of the centre.

9 Turn over. Note FGHI. Lift F . . .

10 . . . and pull it up between A and B, as far as it will go. Repeat with G H and I, still keeping hold of the centre.

11 Turn over.

12 Note JKLM. Lift J . . .

13 . . . and pull it up in front of A. Repeat with K L and M.

14 The Waterlily is complete.

DISH

The Dish is unique in origami: it is the only known *circular* design. What's more, the final shape is very attractive and the opening out moves in Steps 11–12 are particularly satisfying. Use a 6–8 in (15–20 mm) square of paper. For a decorative effect, use a paper differently coloured on its two sides.

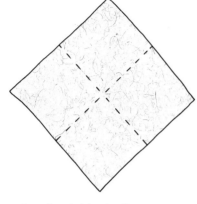

1 Valley fold in half horizontally and vertically, to make four squares. Unfold each crease.

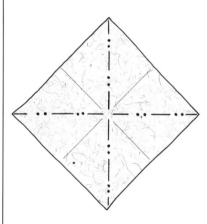

2 Mountain fold each diagonal. Unfold.

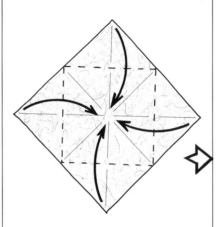

3 Fold the corners to the centre.

4 Fold the corners back out to the edge.

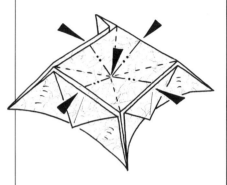

5 Crease and unfold four mountain folds as shown. (It is probably easier to make valley folds by turning the paper over.)

6 Make short mountain diagonals. Pinch the edges near the corners . . .

7 . . . to raise a table shape in the centre and make the paper 3D. Push down on the centre point whilst pushing the edges of the "table" towards the centre . . .

8 . . . like this. Note the X shape of the paper. Flatten the X shape with two points to either side.

9 Reverse fold the front corners inside.

10 Repeat behind.

11 Push the bottom edge upwards with a curved crease, so that the top edges of the pocket separate in a curved shape.

12 This is the result. Repeat on the other three sides.

13 The Dish complete. Neaten the interior edges to make an attractive star shaped central pocket.

FLAPPING BIRD

Here is perhaps the greatest of all "action models". The bird shape is itself satisfying, but the wide, graceful arc made by the wings when flapped is dramatic and appealing. If you want to carry an origami design in your handbag or wallet to entertain people with, this must surely be the one. Use a 6–10 in (15–25 cm) square of paper.

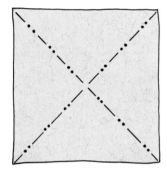

1 Mountain fold both diagonals. Unfold.

2 Valley fold horizontally and vertically. Unfold.

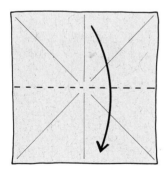

3 Fold the top edge down to the bottom along the existing crease.

4 Hold as shown. Swing your hands together . . .

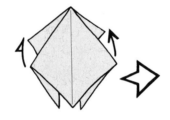

5 . . . to create this 3D star shape. If the pattern of mountains and valleys is incorrect it will not form, so check Steps 1–2.

6 With the closed (neat) corner at the top, fold in the lower front edges to the centre crease . . .

7 . . . like this. Fold down the top triangle.

8 Pull out the side triangles.

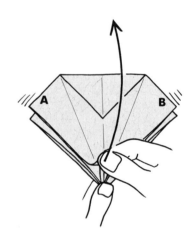

9 Take hold of just the top layer. Lift it upwards . . .

10 . . . swivelling it right up and over the top edge of the paper shape. A and B will move inwards.

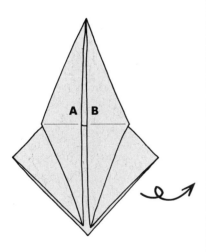

11 Flatten the diamond shape with strong creases. Turn over.

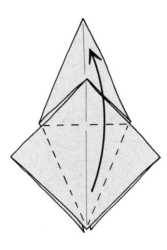

12 Repeat Steps 6–11 on this side, to make another diamond shape to match the first. Note the loose triangle hidden between them.

13 Reverse fold each of the lower points, so that each reverse starts a little below the centre of the diamond.

14 Reverse the head.

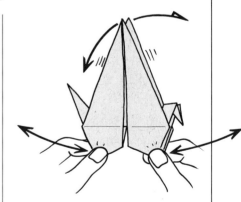

15 Hold as shown. To complete the Flapping Bird, move your hands gently apart and together, apart and together, and the wings will flap!

CRANE

The Crane is the one design that all Japanese people seem to know. In recent times it has become a potent symbol of peace and friendship. Garlands of Cranes strung together in the flat form seen in Step 4 can be seen at many Peace shrines around the world. Use thin or medium-weight paper at least 6 in (15 cm) square. Begin by folding the Flapping Bird up to Step 13.

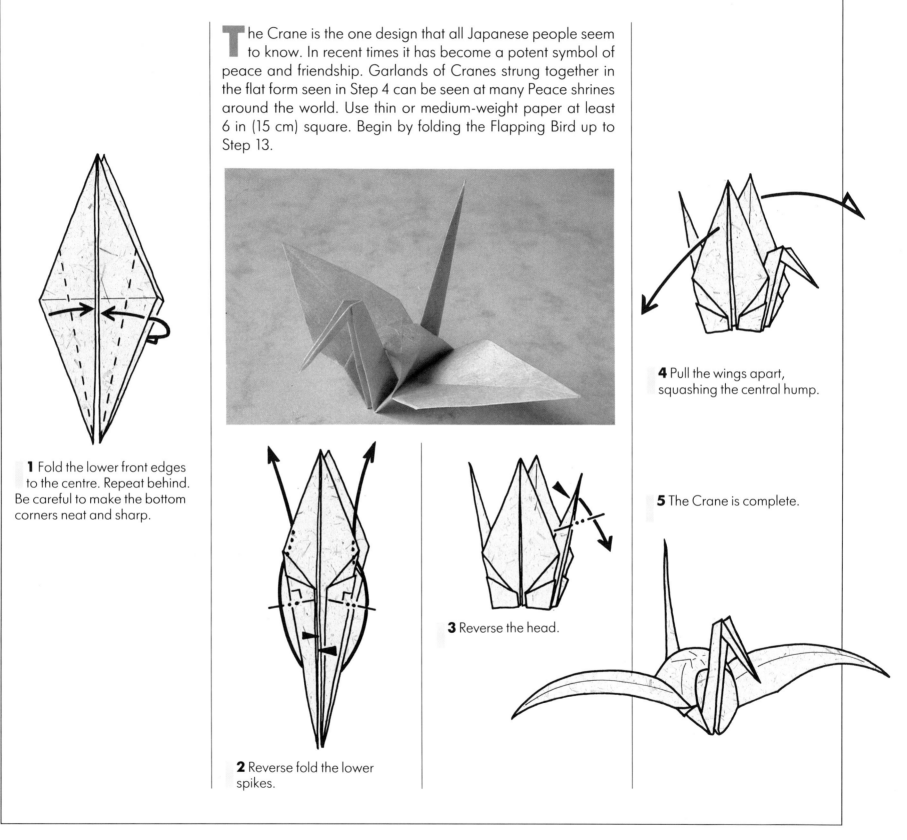

1 Fold the lower front edges to the centre. Repeat behind. Be careful to make the bottom corners neat and sharp.

2 Reverse fold the lower spikes.

3 Reverse the head.

4 Pull the wings apart, squashing the central hump.

5 The Crane is complete.

GLIDER

W hat could be simpler – a Glider with only *two* folds! Be careful to follow the instructions carefully, because it is important to hold and release it in the correct way. There is probably an even simpler Glider with just *one* crease, waiting to be designed! Use a 6 in (15 cm) square of thin paper such as origami paper, airmail paper or undercopy (bank) typing paper. Heavier paper will not float the design through the air.

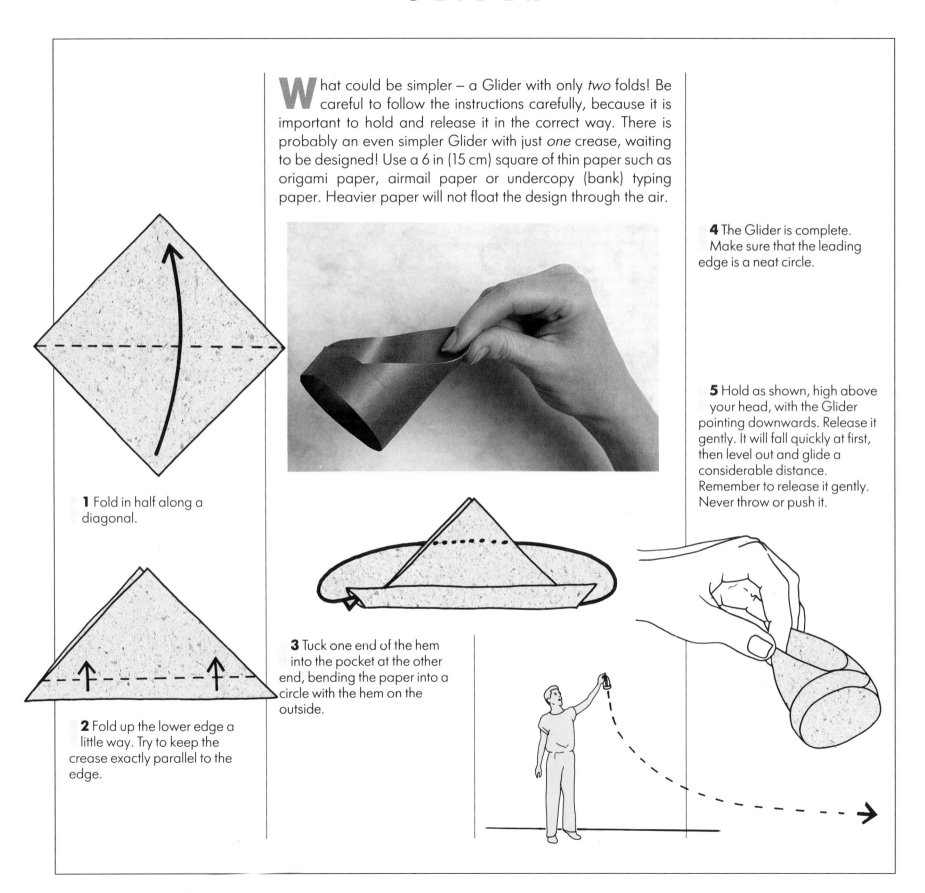

1 Fold in half along a diagonal.

2 Fold up the lower edge a little way. Try to keep the crease exactly parallel to the edge.

3 Tuck one end of the hem into the pocket at the other end, bending the paper into a circle with the hem on the outside.

4 The Glider is complete. Make sure that the leading edge is a neat circle.

5 Hold as shown, high above your head, with the Glider pointing downwards. Release it gently. It will fall quickly at first, then level out and glide a considerable distance. Remember to release it gently. Never throw or push it.

SAMPAN

This design has a remarkable climax when, at Steps 10–12, the entire shape is turned inside-out to suddenly reveal the completed Sampan. A few other designs contain inversions to part of their structure, but none to this extent. A simpler variation is to regard Step 5 as a flat, uncreased square, then to proceed as diagrammed, but omitting Step 13 to create a boat without a canopy. Use a 6–8 in (15–20 cm) square of paper with different colours on the two sides. Begin by creasing both diagonals, then folding a pair of opposite corners to the middle.

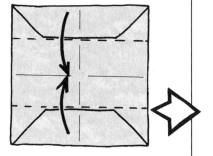

5 Fold the top and bottom edges to the centre.

1 Tuck the corners inside.

2 Turn over.

3 Fold the remaining corners to the centre.

4 Similarly, tuck these corners inside.

6 Turn in the triangles.

7 Narrow one end, then . . .

9 Fold the side corners to the centre.

11 . . . like this. Keep the layers pressed together. Turn over.

13 . . . like this. Lift up the canopies.

14 The Sampan is complete.

8 . . . narrow the other.

10 Pull the side layers right apart to expose a clean base . .

12 The arrowed corners point towards you. Push them down with considerable force, so that they invert backwards and the Sampan turns inside-out . . .

JUNK

The sequence of folds to make the Junk is regarded by many as the most beautiful in all origami, particularly the transformations in Step 2, Steps 5–7, Steps 13–15 and Steps 19–20. Note how the sequence progresses effortlessly from one step to the next like notes in a melody or steps in a ballet, topped by the final extraordinary opening out climax. Use a 6–8 in (15–20 cm) square of paper with different colours on the two sides. Begin with Step 1 of the Sampan (see page 124).

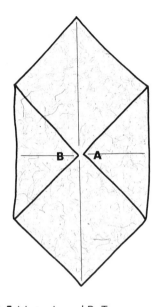

1 Note A and B. Turn over.

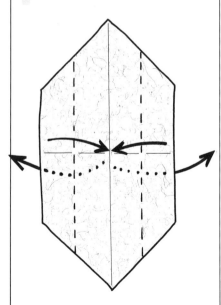

2 Fold the sides to the centre, so that A and B flip to the front . . .

3 . . . like this. Mountain fold the lower portion behind.

4 Pre-crease as shown, through all layers.

5 Fold dot to dot, left and right. This will open the slit down the centre and swivel C downward by a considerable distance.

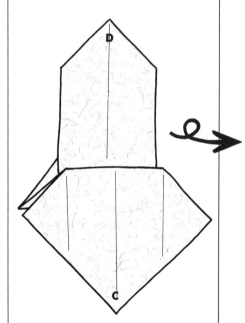

6 Note the position of C. Turn over.

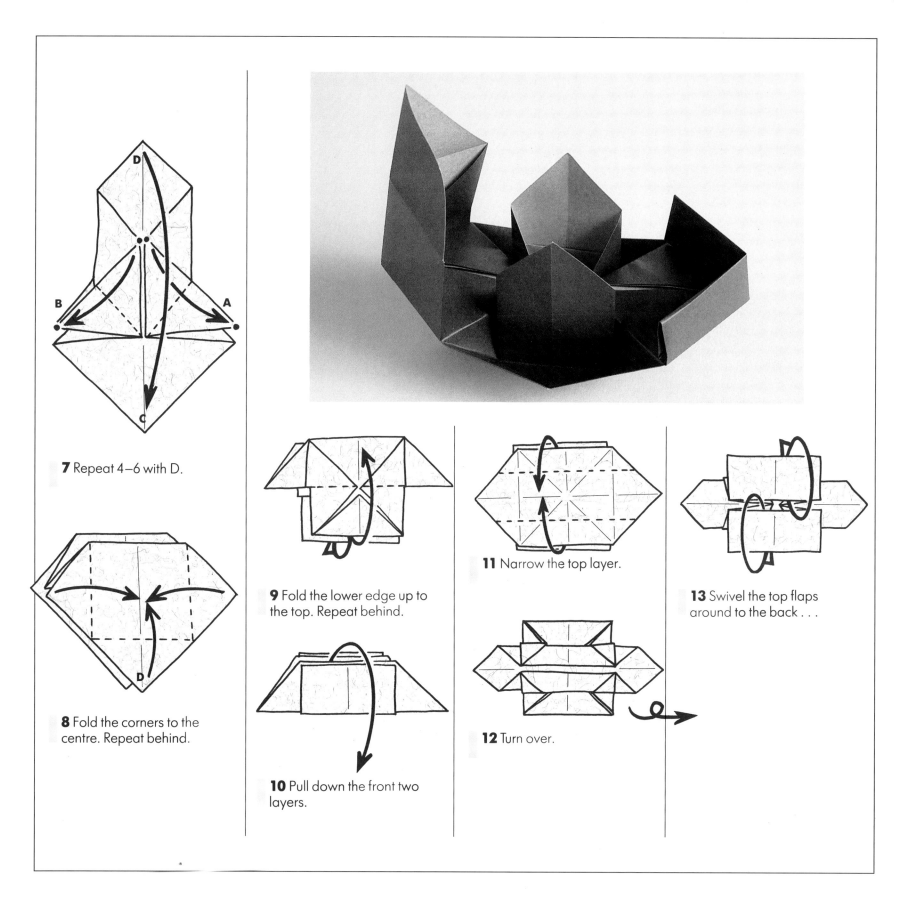

7 Repeat 4–6 with D.

8 Fold the corners to the centre. Repeat behind.

9 Fold the lower edge up to the top. Repeat behind.

10 Pull down the front two layers.

11 Narrow the top layer.

12 Turn over.

13 Swivel the top flaps around to the back . . .

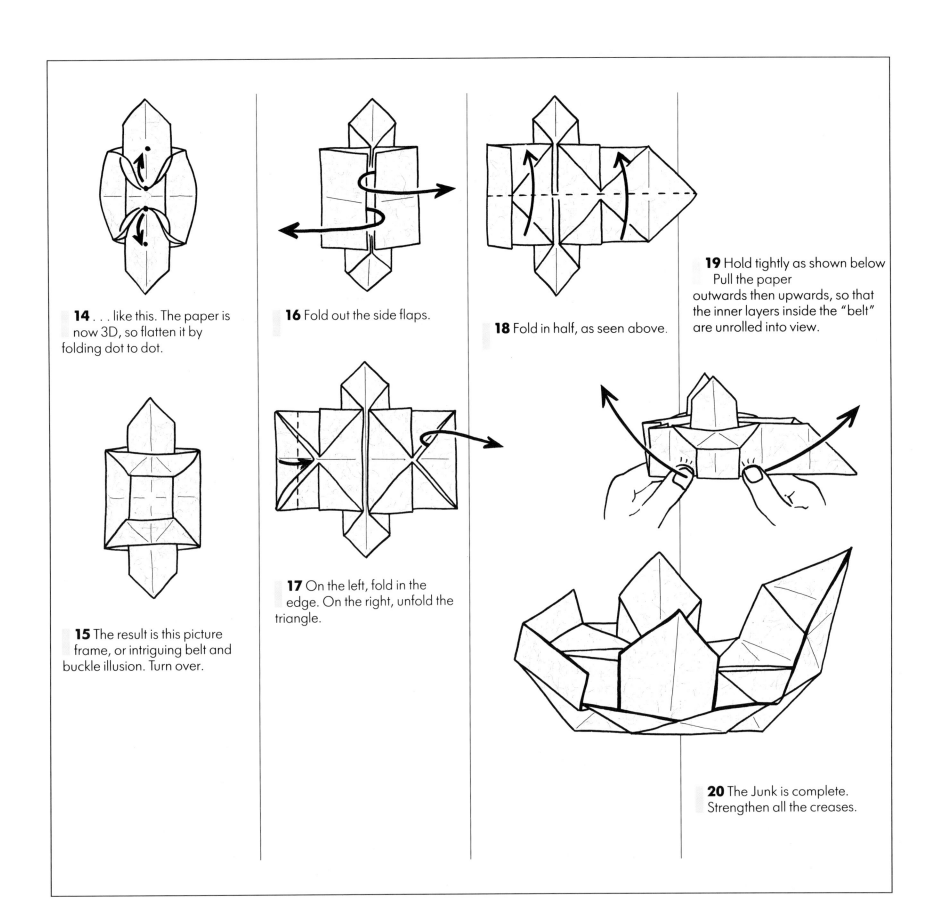

14 . . . like this. The paper is now 3D, so flatten it by folding dot to dot.

15 The result is this picture frame, or intriguing belt and buckle illusion. Turn over.

16 Fold out the side flaps.

17 On the left, fold in the edge. On the right, unfold the triangle.

18 Fold in half, as seen above.

19 Hold tightly as shown below Pull the paper outwards then upwards, so that the inner layers inside the "belt" are unrolled into view.

20 The Junk is complete. Strengthen all the creases.

EASTERN DESIGNS

Origami is the Japanese word for "paper-folding" and is used around the world as a tribute to the original home of the art, some 1500 years ago. The best contemporary designs reveal qualities typical of oriental arts and crafts – elegance, stylization and, in designs of living creatures, more regard for character than for form. The wide range of beautiful papers (the country is renowned for its papers) often mean that more attention is given to the *look* of a design than to its sequence of folds, so that the artistry lies more in the relationships between the paper, the subject and the manipulative finesse of the folder, than in the ballet of the sequence. These designs – particularly those of living creatures by the greatest of origami masters, Akira Yoshizawa – are uncannily alive, but are almost unreproduceable by we lesser folders who do not have "the spirit". Fortunately, though, for books such as this, there is a large body of work that can be reproduced by the lay folder in conventional papers.

In recent years, a less emotive, more geometric style of folding has emerged, drawing not a little inspiration from the technological advances made in the West since the 1950s. The Cube and Stretch Wall are examples of this style.

Outside Japan, there are known to be creative folders in Hong Kong, Singapore and Malaysia.

YOSHIZAWA'S BUTTERFLIES

Akira Yoshizawa is the single most important paper-folder in the world. He was born in 1911, at a time when origami meant little more to the Japanese than the mechanical reproduction of a few traditional designs, and when creative origami was virtually unknown. As with many children, origami became an absorbing hobby of his. Unlike other children though, it later became such an obsession that at the age of 26 he left his job in an iron foundry (where he had usefully learnt the principles of geometry) to devote himself to origami. For a decade he worked alone and in poverty, inventing many new designs and forging his philosophy of creative origami. Shortly before World War II, a twist of fate brought him much publicity and an influential patron to guide him on his professional career.

After the war, Yoshizawa resumed his career, publishing his first book in 1952, establishing the International Origami Center in 1954 and first exhibiting in Europe in 1955. Since then, he has received many cultural honours and travelled widely, including several visits to the West where origami enthusiasts have acclaimed his work.

Yoshizawa separates origami into two kinds: "recreational" and "art". The former he largely dismisses as being the mechanical reproduction of a design to give an illustrative likeness of a subject, but without expression or character. Such designs include all traditional and geometric work and almost all other modern creative work, from East or West. To Yoshizawa, these designs may be clever, but they are without spirit. He advocates an origami which reveals the inner character of the subject through the interpretive skills of the paper folder. Mere symbolic representation is not enough: the folder must have an empathy for the subject he is folding and the material he uses (the paper). If this suggests a philosophy that is too all-embracing and too emotional to be practised by the reader who wishes his origami to simply be an enjoyable pastime, then it is a measure of Yoshizawa's complete commitment to his art.

However total or controversial Yoshizawa's approach may be, there can be no doubting the quality of his work, the range and diversity of which is legendary. In particular, his finesse with paper is without equal. It is so exquisite as to defy reproduction by any other folder. Diagrams can only show the bare bones of a design, which the folder through dedicated practice must flesh out and bring to life.

The butterflies photographed here (which have all been folded by Yoshizawa and generously donated for use in the book) show a good cross-section of his work, from the very simple to the very complex, but all beautifully folded. The simpler ones can be folded by anybody, even young children. Although they are examples of the "recreational" style which he does not usually support, they can be made to flutter wher the central ridge is depressed, bringing them to life and so earning them a place in his renowned teaching performances.

The more complex ones show his engineering prowess. Were this a Yoshizawa book, the designs would be yet more beautiful, but western writers are not usually permitted to publish the very best of his work. Indeed, visitors to his home-cum-studio in Tokyo say that the most extraordinary of his pieces remain unpublished.

It is possible to conceive that a modern origami movement would have evolved without Yoshizawa, but his genius has enriched the art for all time.

YOSHIZAWA'S BUTTERFLY

Here are the instructions for Yoshizawa's best-known Butterfly, drawn by the creator for use in the book and reproduced without alterations or additions. This butterfly is the logo of the International Origami Center, which Yoshizawa founded to help spread friendship and peace through origami. The design is so well-known that it has almost become traditional.

Yoshizawa does not give the written step by step instructions as we have done in other designs, but by now the reader should be familiar enough with the diagrams and symbols to be able to follow his instructions.

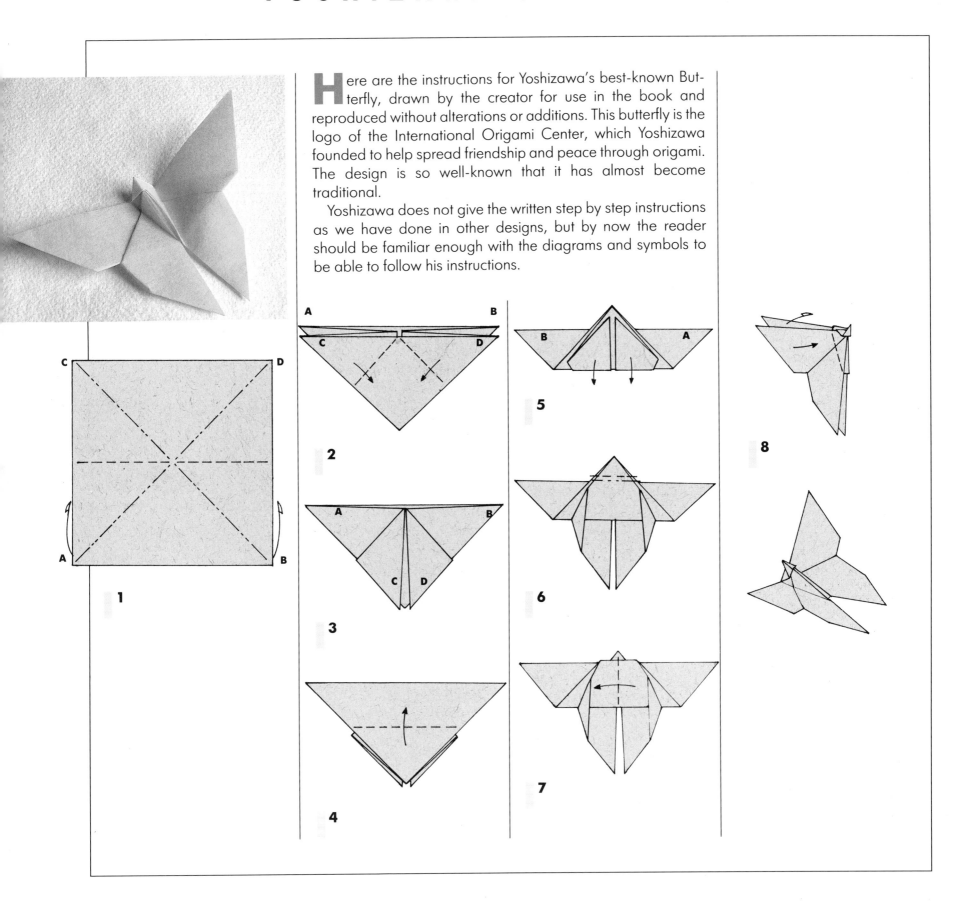

MOUNT FUJI AND THE SEA

The late creator of this design, Seiryo Takegawa (Japan), specialized in producing very simple designs for children, including many wonderful action toys. This little-known masterpiece is typical of his work: simple, poetic, audacious and charming. Perhaps it is like the traditional Bird on page 114 – more a symbol than a representation. Use a 6–8 in (15–20 cm) square. Origami paper is ideal.

1 Fold in half. Unfold.

2 Fold down the top edge a little way, more on the left than on the right.

3 Mountain fold the top corners behind, so that the vertical edges are brought down level with the horizontal fold.

4 Divide the lower section into quarters. All the creases must be valleys.

5 Place mountains between the valleys. Pleat the creases, including the original horizontal fold.

6 Mount Fuji and the Sea complete.

YACHT

There are many origami yachts, boats and ships, but none are as simple or as full of movement as this wonderful design by Japan's First Lady of origami, Mrs Toshie Takahama. Mrs Takahama has produced many exquisite designs, particularly of animals (see her Cat on pages 138–9) and flowers. She has written several books, some of which have recently been translated into English. Use a 6–8 in (15–20 cm) square of origami paper.

1 Fold in the top edge one third of the way towards the diagonal crease.

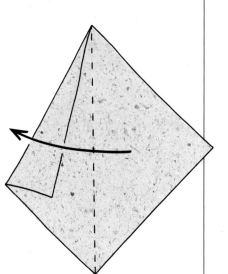

2 Fold the right hand corner across to the left.

3 Fold it back along a crease which starts just to the left of the top corner and goes to the mid-point of the lower edge.

4 Fold the bottom corner across to the right.

5 Mountain fold the bottom corner behind.

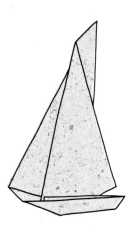

6 The Yacht complete.

ETERNALLY OPENING ORIGAMI

This design is Step 13 of the Flapping Bird (see page 120) turned upside down. It is nothing more than the classic Bird Base, familiar to all experienced folders. What makes it remarkable is that no one until Takuji Sugimura of Japan realized that it could perform the addictive dance described here. The lesson, of course, is never to disregard the familiar in case it holds a wonderful secret. Use 6–8 in (15–20 cm) square of paper.

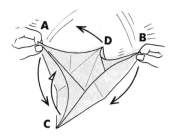

1 Hold points A and B. Separate your hands, moving them outwards and downwards, allowing C and D to rise . . .

2 . . . like this. Begin to bring A and B back together below C and D . . .

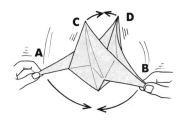

3 . . . like this. Continue until A and B are together at the bottom.

4 The movement complete. Strengthen the creases.

5 Transfer your hands to C and D and repeat Steps 1–4.

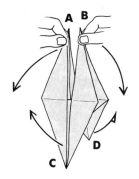

6 Transfer your hands back to A and B and repeat and repeat and repeat! Be careful at Step 2 not to pull A and B too far apart, or the paper will "snap" and lock to look like Step 2 of the Daffodil stem on pages 164–5.

CUBE

The creator of the Cube, Shuzo Fujimoto (Japan) has conducted a great deal of research into the geometry of folding, including important discoveries about how to fold accurate polygons (pentagons, hexagons, and so on) from a square; how to divide an edge into accurate thirds, fifths, etc without "guesstimating"; and how to fold a one-piece solid such as a tetrahedron or an icosahedron. If all this sounds rather dry (it isn't!), just enjoy folding his Cube. In particular, enjoy Step 5 – surely one of the 'best moves' in all origami. Use a 6–8 in (15–20 cm) square of thin or medium weight paper.

1 Carefully divide the paper into quarters, horizontally and vertically, to create 16 squares.

2 Re-crease the creases to look like the pattern of mountains and valleys shown here.

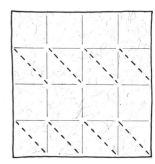

3 Add eight short diagonals. Be precise.

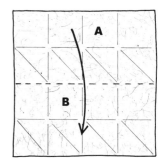

4 Fold in half. Note squares A and B.

5 Hold as shown. Note square A at the front and B behind. The aim is now to slide A up and to the left so that it exactly covers B. When this has happened, the paper will have curled into a cube form. All of the marked creases *must* form cleanly and simultaneously. There is a knack to this "slide", so please try it several times.

6 Tuck the front square inside to lock the top.

7 Turn over.

8 Fold in the corner.

9 Push in the next corner to form part of the lid.

10 Push in the next corner . . .

11 . . . and the next.

12 Tuck the triangle inside the cube to lock the top.

13 The Cube complete.

CAT

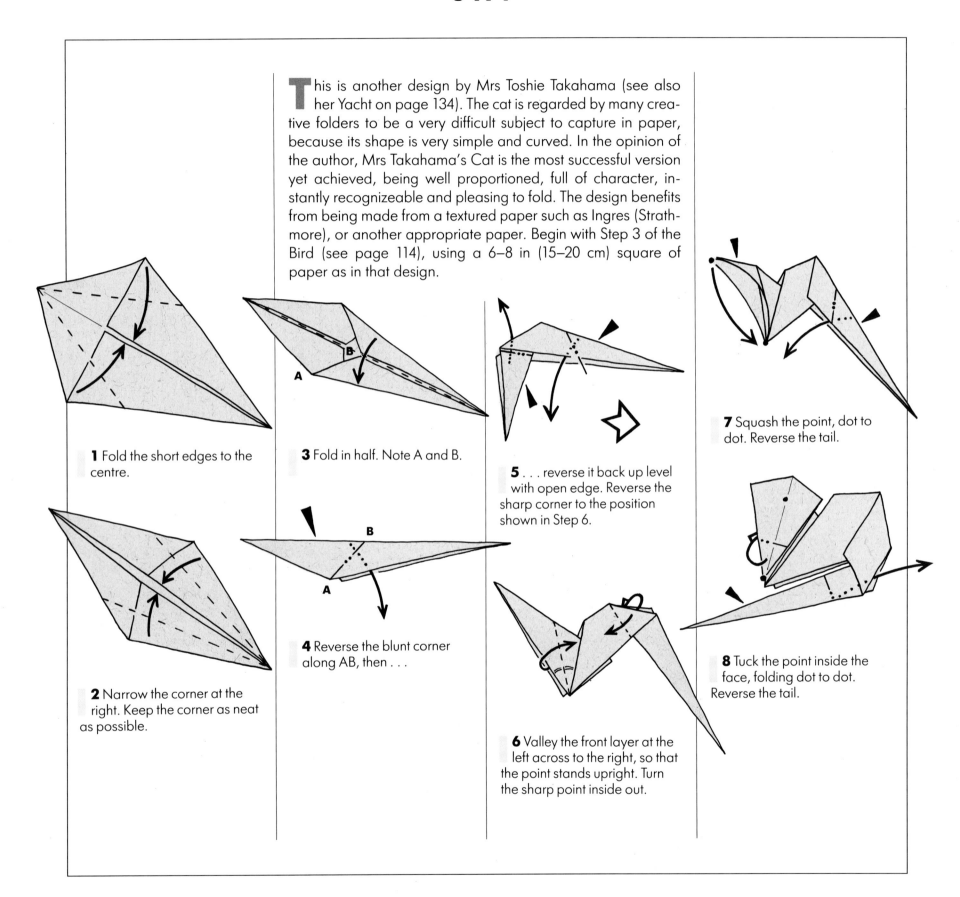

This is another design by Mrs Toshie Takahama (see also her Yacht on page 134). The cat is regarded by many creative folders to be a very difficult subject to capture in paper, because its shape is very simple and curved. In the opinion of the author, Mrs Takahama's Cat is the most successful version yet achieved, being well proportioned, full of character, instantly recognizeable and pleasing to fold. The design benefits from being made from a textured paper such as Ingres (Strathmore), or another appropriate paper. Begin with Step 3 of the Bird (see page 114), using a 6–8 in (15–20 cm) square of paper as in that design.

1 Fold the short edges to the centre.

2 Narrow the corner at the right. Keep the corner as neat as possible.

3 Fold in half. Note A and B.

4 Reverse the blunt corner along AB, then . . .

5 . . . reverse it back up level with open edge. Reverse the sharp corner to the position shown in Step 6.

6 Valley the front layer at the left across to the right, so that the point stands upright. Turn the sharp point inside out.

7 Squash the point, dot to dot. Reverse the tail.

8 Tuck the point inside the face, folding dot to dot. Reverse the tail.

9 Fold the ears forward.
Reverse the hind legs.
Outside reverse the tail.

10 Shape the nose. Fold the
top of the head behind.

11 Fold up the ears.

12 The Cat complete.

INCENSE BURNER

The Reverend Philip Shen (Hong Kong) specializes in creating geometric designs which collapse into shape from a carefully laid out pattern of pre-creases. The Incense Burner is one of his finest designs, particularly because the final shape is conjured from a very familiar pattern of pre-creases — the kite shape in Step 2 is known to all paper-folders, yet simply to repeat it on each corner and add the central star shape is enough to create a beautiful design. Use a 6–10 in (15–20 cm) square of medium-weight paper.

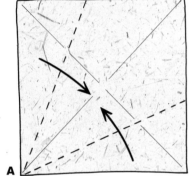

1 Fold the two edges meeting at A to the centre crease.

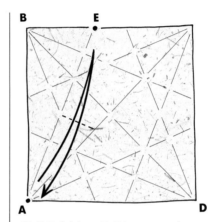

3 Repeat with the other two edges meeting at C.

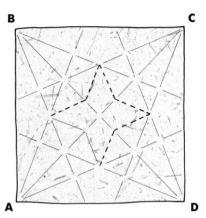

5 Fold A to E, E being at the end of the upper crease made in Step 1. Crease *only* where shown.

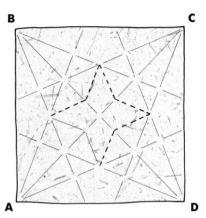

7 Repeat with B C and D, making 6 more short creases.

2 Unfold.

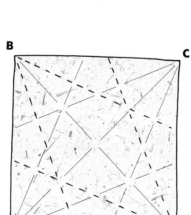

4 Repeat with the two edges meeting at B, then those meeting at D.

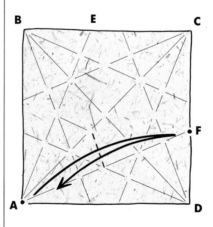

6 Repeat, folding A to F, F being at the end of the lower crease made in Step 1.

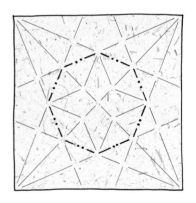

8 Re-crease the octagon with mountain creases.

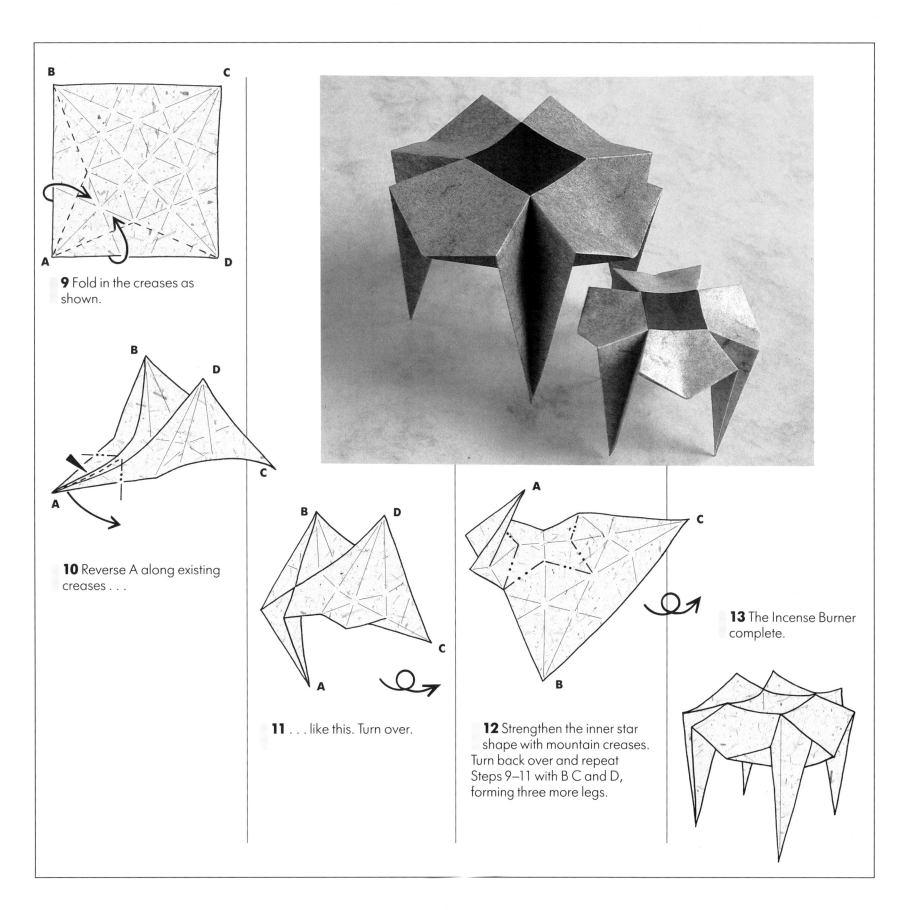

9 Fold in the creases as shown.

10 Reverse A along existing creases . . .

11 . . . like this. Turn over.

12 Strengthen the inner star shape with mountain creases. Turn back over and repeat Steps 9–11 with B C and D, forming three more legs.

13 The Incense Burner complete.

TULIP AND STEM

Here is the first two-piece design in the book and one of the simplest and most appealing of all origami flowers. Its creator, Kunihiko Kasahara (Japan), has written over 100 origami books – including some in English – which feature his own prolific output. To make the Tulip and Stem, make the Tulip square half the size of the Stem square, so that (for example) if the Tulip is made from a 4 in (10 cm) square, the Stem is made from an 8 in (20 cm) square. The Tulip begins with Step 6 of the Flapping Bird (see page 120) turned upside down and the Stem begins with Step 3 of the Bird (see page 114).

BLOOM

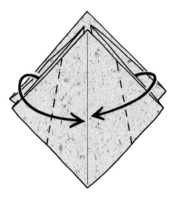

1 With the open corner at the top, fold the front corners to the centre crease. Note that the creases taper towards the top. Repeat behind.

2 Unfold.

3 Fold the open edges to the crease. Repeat behind.

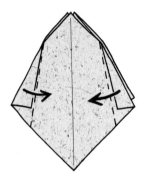

4 Fold over along Step 1 creases. Repeat behind.

5 With a pair of scissors, snip off the tip. Snip off less than you think you should – the hole can be enlarged with another snip, but cannot be made smaller!

6 Open out.

7 The Bloom complete.

STEM

1 Fold the short edges to the centre crease.

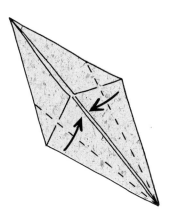

2 Narrow the bottom corner. Keep it neat.

3 Fold in half, dot to dot.

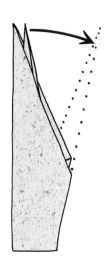

4 Pull the sharp point out to the dotted position. Squeeze the paper flat at the bottom to let the sharp point retain its new position.

5 The Stem complete. Insert the sharp spike into the base of the Bloom.

143

FOX

The stylization typical of Japanese designs is shown to good effect in this design by Mitsue Okuda. What's more, although the front and back are folded differently (the tail is to one side), the design looks good from all angles. The head is a particularly interesting feature of the design, being so remarkably simple. Use an oblong of thin or medium-weight paper, twice as long as it is wide, for instance 4–8 in (10–20 cm).

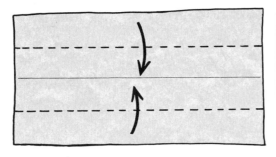

1 Fold the long edges to the centre crease.

2 Reverse twice at the left.

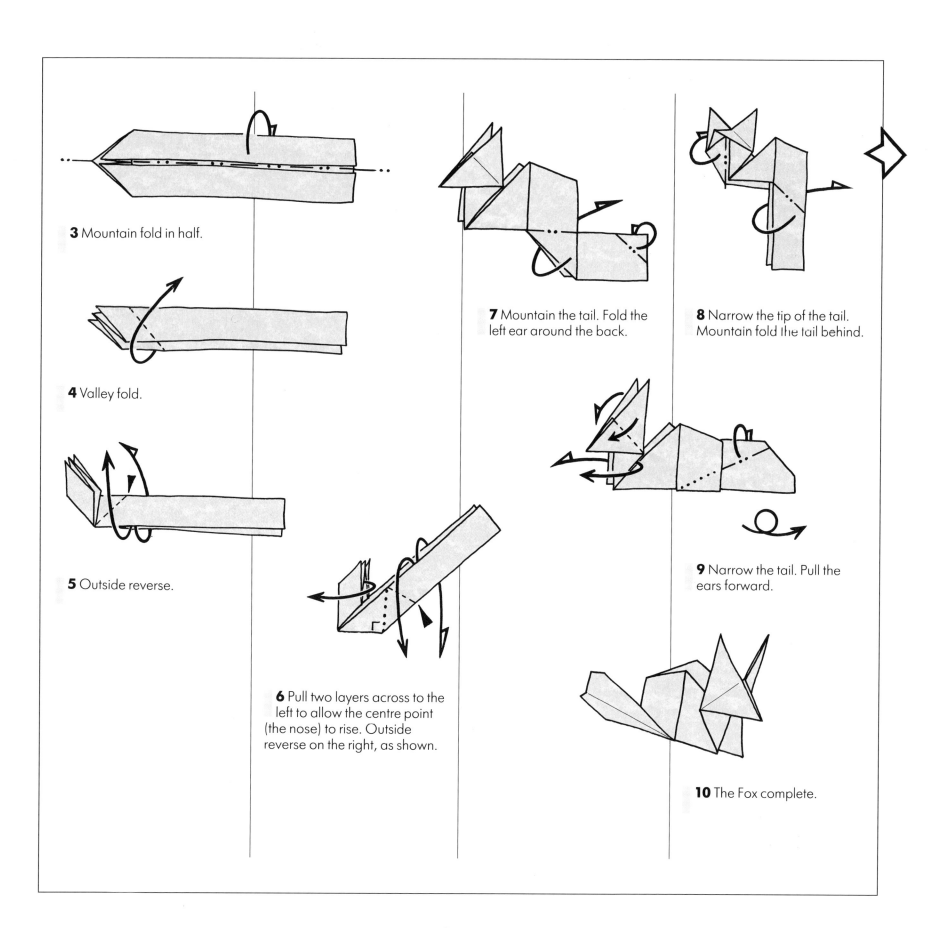

3 Mountain fold in half.

4 Valley fold.

5 Outside reverse.

6 Pull two layers across to the left to allow the centre point (the nose) to rise. Outside reverse on the right, as shown.

7 Mountain the tail. Fold the left ear around the back.

8 Narrow the tip of the tail. Mountain fold the tail behind.

9 Narrow the tail. Pull the ears forward.

10 The Fox complete.

STRETCH WALL

The basic grid made in Step 6 can, with the addition of diagonal creases, be collapsed into any number of geometric patterns, some very complex. This design by Yoshihide Momotani of Japan is one of the most astonishing, being elastic – that is, it can expand and collapse. Also, whereas the front is a horizontal pattern of bricks, the reverse shows the same pattern, but vertically! The design is not difficult, but time-consuming. Fold the grid very carefully and the later folds will fall into place. The final "unpicking" of the edges in Steps 18–20 is a very pretty and dramatic conclusion. Use a sheet of thin or medium-weight paper at least 8 in (20 cm) square.

1 Crease accurate quarters, all valleys.

2 Crease accurate eighths, all valleys.

3 Place mountains midway between the valleys. Turn over and rotate the paper.

4 Check that the top crease is a valley (if it isn't, turn the paper over so that it is).

5 Repeat Steps 1–3, creasing valleys as quarters and eighths, then mountains in between . . .

6 . . . to make this grid.

7 Make pleats where shown . . .

8 . . . like this. Turn the paper over and rotate.

9 Pleat again.

10 The pleats complete. Note A B and C. Fold dot to dot, so that the lower pleat swivels downwards . . .

11 . . . like this. Note the diagonal crease which has to be made *beneath* the vertical pleat to accommodate the swivel.

12 The swivel and hidden diagonal creases complete.

13 Repeat the swivel with A D and E.

14 Repeat down the centre, swivelling the pleat upwards to lie level with the top edge.

16 The swivel complete. Repeat three more times down the centre, then four times down the left hand edge.

18 Note FG and HI. Fold edge GH across to the right, so that G separates from F and H separates from I . . .

20 . . . like this. Repeat, unbuttoning more edges to reveal a regular brick pattern.

15 As before, diagonal creases need to be made beneath the vertical pleats, this time one at each end of the swivel.

17 The swivels complete. Turn over.

19 . . . like this. Pull out the paper beneath F and I, so that edge GH can flatten to the right . . .

21 The Stretch Wall complete. Hold opposite edges and pull apart to open the bricks.

WESTERN DESIGNS

Creative origami in the West – as a creative movement, at least – began in the 1950s. A surprising number of traditional designs were known before that time, such as the triangular newspaper hat and the paper dart, but the creative potential of the art had not been explored to any depth. In the 1950s, a few key books, exhibitions and TV programmes established the art, since when it has continued to grow and diversify, perhaps by now surpassing even the Japanese for innovation.

There are now many styles of folding, created by enthusiasts who fold for many reasons: for some it is a decorative craft, or perhaps a form of puzzle solving, for others it is an exploration of geometry, a way to relax, an aid to teaching or simply because the possibility of folding a sheet of paper into a recognizable form is an extraordinary phenomenon which rarely fails to amaze or please.

The designs in this chapter show the preoccupation of most western creative folders with engineering and geometry, rather than the artistry of the eastern designers. These designs are complex (some fearsomely so) but for reasons of space, few are included here. Instead, the chapter presents some of the simpler classics. For those who would like to fold complex designs, many can be found in books published in the United States by Engel, Montroll, Lang and Weiss.

ARROW

Some designs are so simple and seemingly so obvious that they appear to have been "discovered", rather than "created". It is almost as though they were there all the time. To see these designs in the paper demands an original approach, not just a reworking of familiar techniques. This design by Tun Ken Lamb (England) may not be to your taste, but its originality is startling. Use a square of paper of any size differently coloured on the two sides.

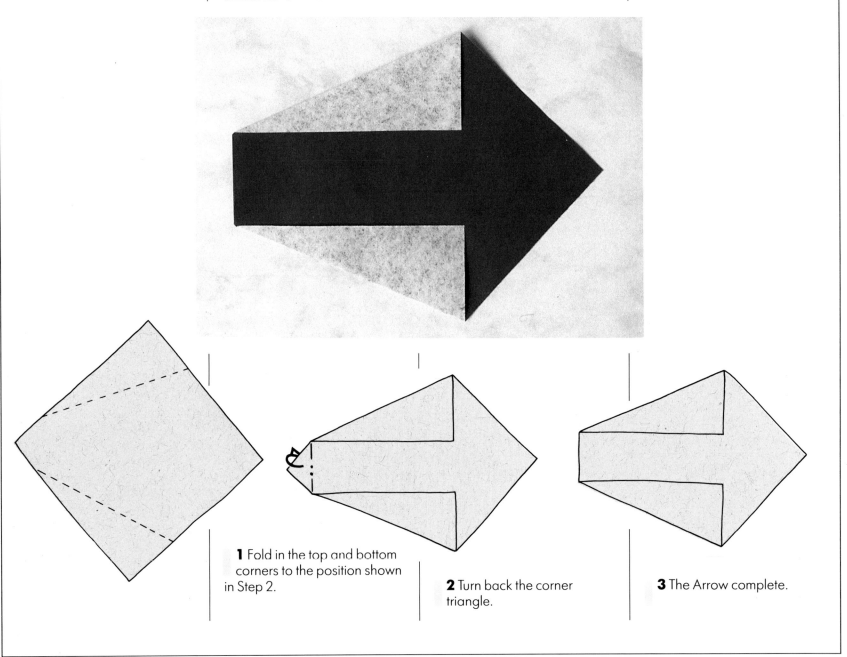

1 Fold in the top and bottom corners to the position shown in Step 2.

2 Turn back the corner triangle.

3 The Arrow complete.

SNAP HEXAHEDRON

Hexahedrons are common in origami. This one by Edwin Corrie (England) is one of the simplest and features an interesting move at Step 5. To make the 3 × 3 grid of squares needed in Step 1, fold a 4 × 4 grid by creasing halves and quarters horizontally and vertically, then cut off a line of squares along two adjacent edges to leave a 3 × 3 grid. Use a 6 in (15 cm) square of paper. Large squares will not "snap" at Step 7.

1 Fold the vertical diagonal as a mountain and the horizontal diagonal as a valley.

2 Fold dot to dot. Unfold.

3 Similarly, fold dot to dot. Unfold.

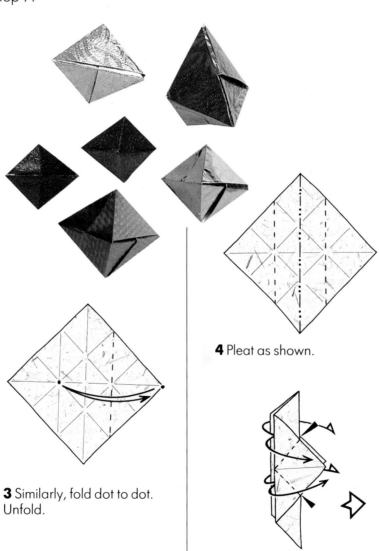

4 Pleat as shown.

5 Outside reverse the top and bottom corners.

6 Valley fold the top corner into the pocket formed by the lower outside reverse fold. Then, mountain the lower corner into the upper outside reverse fold, behind.

7 Hold as shown and squeeze. The left hand corners will separate to create a third edge around the middle, forming a 3D hexahedron.

8 The Snap Hexahedron complete.

THE UN-UNFOLDABLE BOX

Boxes are the most common subject in origami. Some are very complex and ornate, whereas this one by Ed Sullivan (USA) is particularly plain. However, the fascination of this design *is in the folding*, because once folded, it cannot then be unfolded, at least not without making extra folds or fumbling with the paper. It is unique in origami and a remarkable design. Use a large square of medium-weight paper.

1 Pinch the mid-points of the four edges. Use them as a guide to make four valley creases along the horizontal and vertical quarter marks.

2 Make mountain folds midway between the valley quarters and the edges.

3 Form valley diagonals at the corners, to create a box with triangular flaps.

4 Point two flaps to the left and two to the right. Fold the triangles in half by turning the loose corners inside.

5 Fold the triangles to the inside, flat against the box.

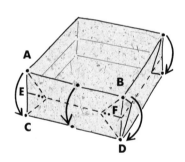

6 Collapse, bringing A down to C and B down to D. E and F move towards the centre of the front edge. Repeat behind.

7 This is the shape half collapsed . . .

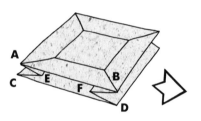

8 . . . and here fully collapsed. Note E and F.

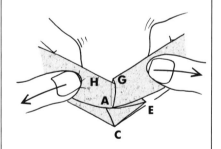

9 Hold corner AC as shown. Pull your hands gently apart and H will slide away from G . . .

10 . . . like this. Keep pulling . . .

11 . . . until the corner is fully formed. Repeat at the other corners of the box.

12 The Un-unfoldable Box complete.

FACE

Many liberties can be taken with the shape of a face before it becomes unrecognizable, which is why origami faces are a particularly interesting subject for creative paper folders. Not all the facial features need be present. This face by Steven Casey (Australia) – for example – does not have a mouth. Other designs may only have a nose, or just the hair, or may be extraordinarily detailed, even sculpted-looking. The shapes for this face are strong and harmonious, and the sequence is clean and flowing. Use a 6–8 in (15–20 cm) square of paper with different colours on the two sides.

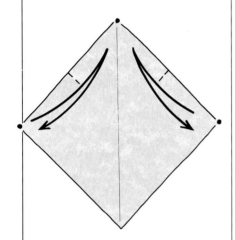

1 Fold the top corner to the left and right corners in turn, pinching the mid-points of the top edges.

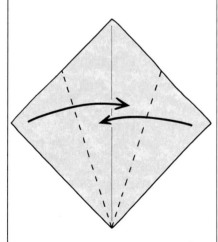

2 Make creases which connect each mid-point with the bottom corner, folding the left and right corners across the middle.

3 Make creases to bisect each of the three angles on the triangular flap, so that the flap collapses to look like Step 4. Repeat on the right.

4 Turn the loose flaps inside-out, so that they change colour.

5 Swivel the triangles inwards so that they meet at the centre.

6 Fold over.

7 Repeat on the left.

8 Reverse (or sink) the bottom point up inside the face, turning the point inside out.

9 Pull the cheeks apart to expose the point just reversed.

10 Form three creases as shown to make the point stand upright . . .

11 . . . like this. Squash it flat.

12 On the left, fold down the loose point of the eye to look like the eye drawn on the other side of the face, then fold it downwards. Blunt the nose. Round off the chin and hair.

13 The Face complete.

ROOSTER

This design by Florence Temko (USA) is a superb example of how a few carefully placed inside and outside reverse folds can create a design with style and character from the very familiar origami shape shown in Step 6 (sometimes called a Fish Base). The design when folded *looks* folded, which, curiously, not all origami does. A design which has clearly been folded without the need to cut or fold pieces together is somehow more satisfying. Use a 6–8 in (15–20 cm) square of medium-weight paper. Crease and unfold both diagonals.

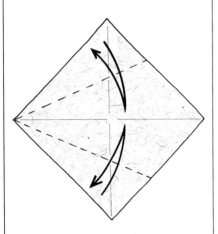

1 Fold the bottom left and top left edges to the centre crease. Unfold.

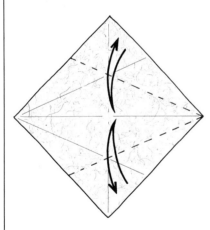

2 Repeat on the right.

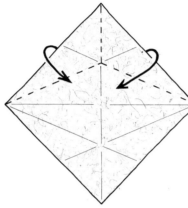

3 Fold in the three creases as shown, so that the top corner stands upright . . .

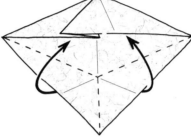

4 . . . like this. Flatten it to the left.

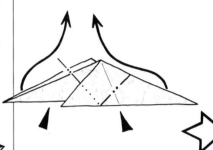

5 Repeat at the bottom, once more flattening the loose corner to the left.

6 Mountain the bottom portion behind.

7 Reverse twice.

8 Reverse.

9 Reverse. Note the angle.

10 Valley, repeat behind.

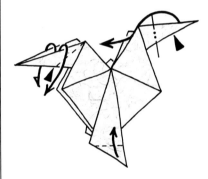

11 At the left, outside reverse. At the right, reverse. Valley the feet. Repeat behind. The valley creases on the feet should be at such an angle that the Rooster can balance.

12 Reverse the beak.

13 The Rooster complete.

POP-UP DOUBLE CUBE

T he late and much missed Eric Kenneway (England) specialized in creating designs which were marvellous to fold but which when complete, did not always look too spectacular. For him, the joy of origami was in the folding, not the looking. His Pop-up Double Cube is perhaps an extreme example of his thesis — it has a fine sequence with intriguing moves at Steps 4–6, Step 11 and the climactic opening at Step 16, but the result *looks* very ordinary. Of its kind, it is a masterpiece. Use a 6–8 in (15–20 cm) square of medium-weight paper.

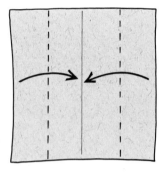

1 Valley the edges to the centre crease.

3 Fold up the triangle.

5 . . . like this. Flatten the paper by bringing the corners together.

7 Fold in half.

2 Mountain the bottom corners behind.

4 Moisten your fingers for a good grip and hold as shown. Pull the outer layers, sliding them out to the sides . . .

6 The move complete. Repeat Steps 2–6 at the top.

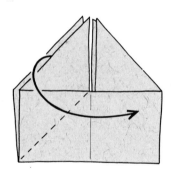

8 Fold across to the right.

9 Pull out the hidden corner.

10 Fold down the triangle.

11 Tuck the loose triangle right into the pocket. Keep it neat.

12 Fold the loose corner up and to the left.

13 The left side is complete. Turn over.

14 Repeat Steps 7–13 on this side.

15 Creasing complete.

16 Hold as shown and pull the central flaps upwards and outwards . . .

17 . . . like this, to form the completed Pop-up Double Cube.

STAR

Origami, like all arts and crafts, is prone to trends. The latest is "modular" folding, in which identical units are folded and interlocked to form flat patterns, solids or stars. Some of these systems are very beautiful, perhaps profound. This Star by Nick Robinson (England) is very simple and particularly elegant in its construction. It need not have 5 points — any number greater than 2 will interlock. For a Star, use at least five sheets of square paper, either all the same colour or all different, depending on your taste. A 3 in (7.5 cm) square is a good size.

MODULE

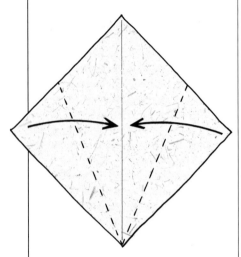

1 Fold the lower edges to the centre crease.

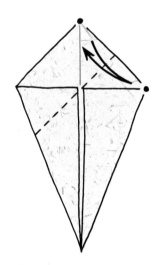

2 Fold dot to dot, as shown.

3 Repeat, but now with the opposite edge.

4 Re-fold Step 3, but this time reverse folding the lower right portion of the crease. Note A.

5 Pull out A to the front.

6 Crease two valleys and a mountain as shown, to give the module some shape . . .

7 . . . like this. The module is complete. For a Star, make four more.

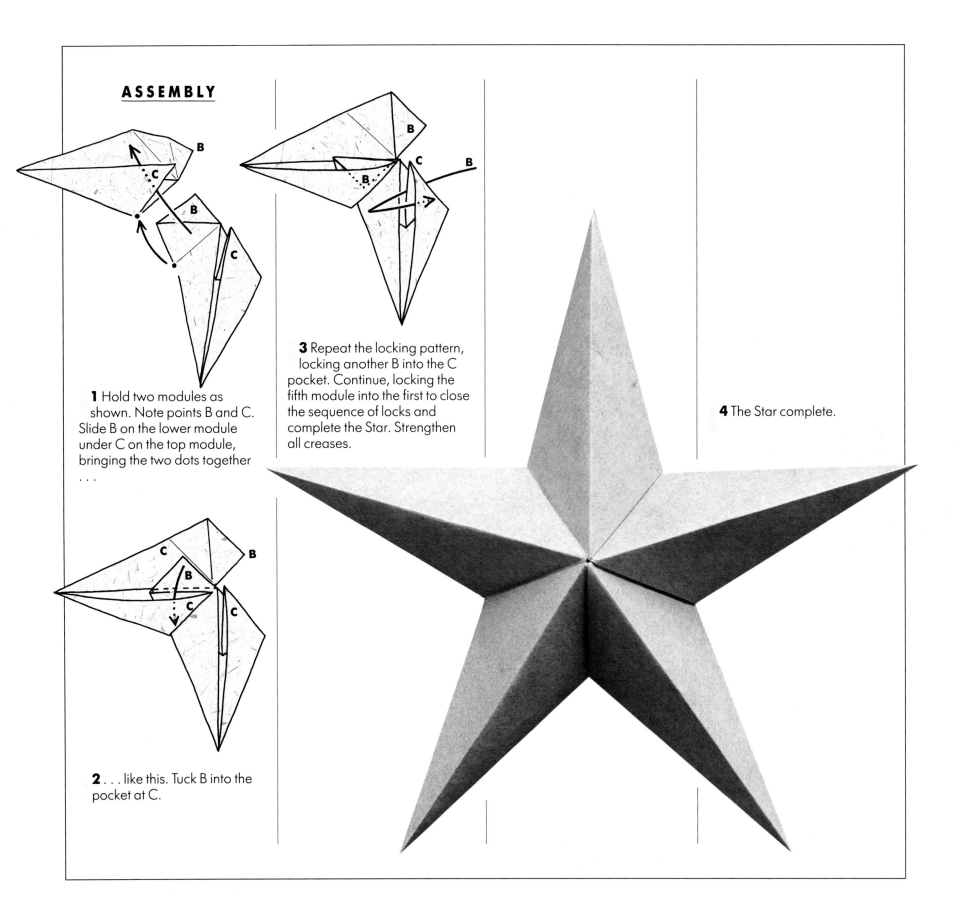

ASSEMBLY

1 Hold two modules as shown. Note points B and C. Slide B on the lower module under C on the top module, bringing the two dots together . . .

2 . . . like this. Tuck B into the pocket at C.

3 Repeat the locking pattern, locking another B into the C pocket. Continue, locking the fifth module into the first to close the sequence of locks and complete the Star. Strengthen all creases.

4 The Star complete.

DAFFODIL

Technically, this design by Ted Norminton (England) is the most advanced in the book and should only be attempted by experienced folders. Compare it with the much simpler Tulip and Stem on page 142 – the two extremes of style show how beauty can be achieved by very different means. Note the intriguing method in Steps 1–6 for folding an accurate hexagon. Persevere with the difficult "sink" at Step 11 – practice will make it much easier. Use a medium-weight yellow square for the bloom and a green square of the same size for the stem. A 10 in (25 cm) square will create a life-size bloom.

BLOOM

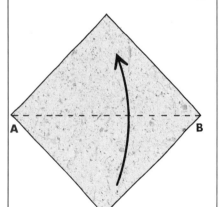

1 Fold in half along a diagonal.

2 Pinch the mid-point and the upper quarter point. Fold the mid-point edge on to the quarter point crease, so that the new crease runs exactly to the centre of the bottom edge. Be very accurate!

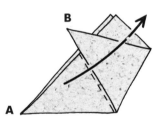

3 Fold the left corner across.

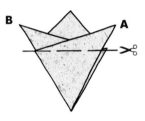

4 Cut off the upper portion of paper as shown.

5 Open out . . .

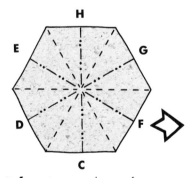

6 . . . to reveal a perfect hexagon! Crease mountains and valleys as shown, collapsing them to make Step 7.

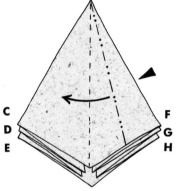

7 If the bottom edge runs straight across, turn the whole shape inside-out to make the shape seen here. Lift F and squash . . .

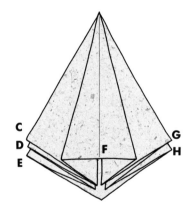

8 . . . like this. Repeat with C D E G and H. When squashing, try to keep the same number of layers left and right.

9 Lift point F along the marked creases (petal fold).

10 Unfold the Step 9 creases. Repeat five more times.

11 Invert or sink the top corner down into the body of the paper, at the level shown. Open out the hexagon to do so, then collapse it back into shape when the rim of the sink has been creased into a continuous mountain crease and the centre inverted. This is a difficult and lengthy procedure, even for experts, so persevere. The effort is worth it!

12 Tuck F up inside the front layer, reversing some of the Step 9 creases. Repeat five more times around the layers.

13 Fold one layer across to the left, to reveal . . .

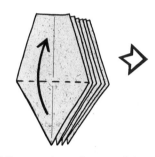

14 . . . a clean face. Fold up the bottom triangle. Repeat five more times around the layers.

15 Fold one layer across . . .

16 . . . to reveal a clean face. Note that for clarity, only the front layer will now be drawn. Crease and unfold as shown.

17 Fold the corners up to the centre crease.

18 Re-fold the Step 16 creases, so that the bottom portion of each crease disappears into the lower triangle.

19 Fold the layer across. Repeat Steps 15–19 five more times. Note I J and K.

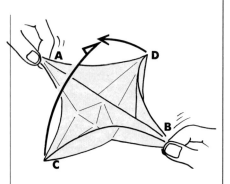

2 . . . like this. Flatten bringing C and D together.

20 Note I J and K again. Fold K behind, so that I and J are brought together and locked. Repeat five more times within the Bloom.

21 Pull down each of the six petals and reverse the rim of the Bloom to shape it.

22 The Bloom complete.

STEM

3 Fold the triangle in half below C, swivelling B downwards.

1 Begin with Step 2 of Eternally Opening Origami on page 135. Hold as shown. Pull A and B smartly apart, until the diagonal which connects them pops into a rigid mountain crease . . .

4 Note the position of B. Turn over.

6 Fold a layer across at the front. Repeat behind but on the opposite side. Rotate the paper upside-down.

8 Push in or sink the bottom corner. Note that the crease tilts upward at the left. Repeat behind.

10 Reverse.

5 Repeat Step 3, swivelling A down to B.

7 Narrow the front layer at the right. Repeat behind.

9 Narrow the flap on the left. Repeat behind.

11 The Stem complete. Insert the spike into the back of the Bloom.

ARCHITECTURAL MODULE

This is not strictly a "modular" design like the Star on page 160, because here there could be several different modules that lock together. The system is very much like a set of children's building blocks, which can be put together in many ways. Make as many as you can, then experiment with them to see what you can make – the photo shows just a few of the possibilities. The system is by Didier Boursin (France). Use squares of medium-weight paper. 4 in (10 cm) squares will work well.

BAR MODULE: END LOCK

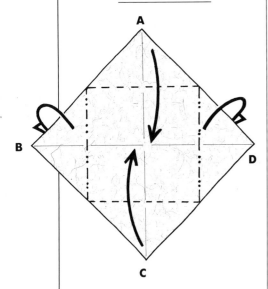

1 Valley corners A and C to the centre. Mountain corners B and D behind to the centre.

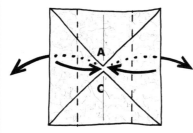

2 Fold the edges to the centre crease, allowing corners B and D to flip to the front.

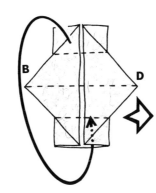

3 Crease three valleys as shown. Tuck the top edge deep inside the pocket at the bottom, locking the module into a triangular shape.

4 The completed module. The protruding triangles can lock into other modules . . .

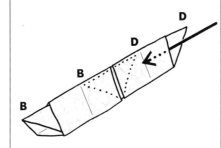

5 . . . like this. The chain can be extended infinitely.

BAR MODULE: SIDE LOCK

1 Begin with Step 2 above. Fold the top and bottom edges to the centre crease.

2 Crease three valleys. Tuck the right hand edge deep inside the pocket at the left edge, locking the module into a triangular shape. Allow corners B and D to flip out.

3 The completed module. The protruding triangles can tuck into other modules . . .

4 . . . like this. The chain can be extended infinitely.

BAR MODULE: END AND SIDE LOCKS

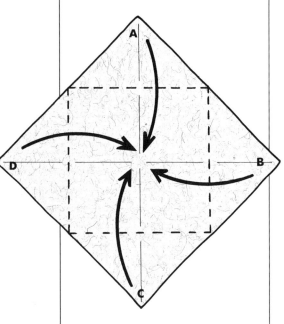

1 Fold the four corners to the middle.

2 Turn over.

3 Fold the top and bottom edges to the centre crease, allowing corners A and C to flip out.

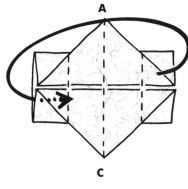

4 Crease three valleys as shown. Tuck the right edge deep into the pocket to lock the module into a triangular shape.

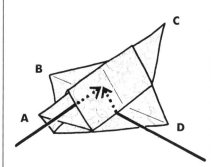

5 The module complete. Other modules can interlock at either end or either side, or both.

FOUR-WAY JUNCTION

1 Begin with Step 3 of the End and Side Locks module above. Fold the bottom edge to the centre crease, allowing C to flip to the front.

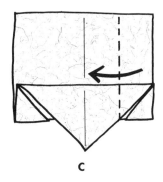

2 Fold the right edge to the centre, allowing D to flip to the front.

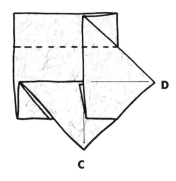

3 Fold the top edge to the centre, allowing A to flip to the front.

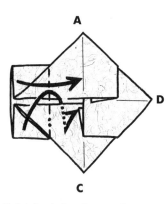

4 Fold the left edge to the centre, allowing B to flip to the front. Reverse the bottom section of the crease, so that . . .

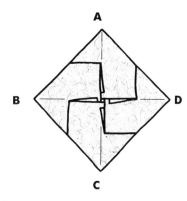

5 . . . the paper is completely symmetrical around the centre point. Turn over.

6 Crease and unfold mountains and valleys as shown, allowing the centre to rise towards you.

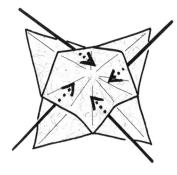

7 The completed module. Each protruding module can interlock with an End Lock module or Corner Junction (below).

CORNER JUNCTION

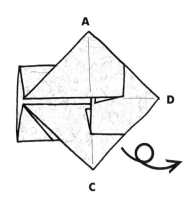

1 Begin with Step 4 of the Four-way Junction module. Turn over.

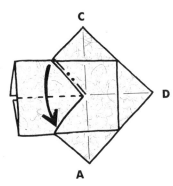

2 Form valley and mountain creases as shown, to make the shape 3D. The centre should rise towards you.

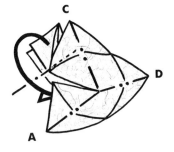

3 Fold the loose square inside the pyramid. Strengthen the creases which run from the apex to corners A C and D.

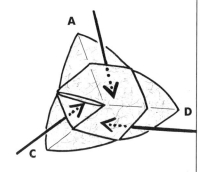

4 The completed module. Each protruding triangle can interlock with an End Lock module or a Four-way Junction.

BARKING DOG

An author should not perhaps include his own work in a book of classic origami, but I have to say that this design gives me great satisfaction. I discovered the action at Step 5 quite by accident whilst playing with the paper and looking for ways to resolve the shape into an acceptable design. From there, the head and tail just folded themselves. Use a 6–8 in (15–20 cm) square of thin or medium-weight paper, differently coloured on the two sides. Start at Step 3 of the Bird on page 114.

1 Mountain fold in half.

2 Reverse fold, to the position shown in Step 3.

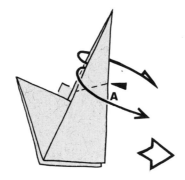

3 Outside reverse fold, to the position shown in Step 4. Note A.

4 Pull out the internal layer at A . . .

5 . . . like this. Repeat behind. Make three reverse folds on the head (the exact placement is unimportant). Pleat the tail.

6 The Barking Dog complete. In this pose it begs.

7 To make it bark, hold as shown and move your left hand to the left and back. The head will move up and down, as though barking!

ROWING BOAT

This design by Martin Wall (England) shows an elegant and concise way to create a simple shape. Steps 8–9 are particularly pleasing moves, not just for the way that they lock the boat into shape, but for the way in which the inside is kept clean. Made from metallic kitchen foil or greaseproof paper it will float. Otherwise, use a 6–8 in (15–20 cm) square of medium-weight paper.

1 Valley into quarters.

2 Turn in the left hand corners, top and bottom.

3 Fold in half.

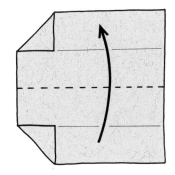

4 Reverse the bottom corners, level with the quarter crease.

5 Open the reverse.

6 Reverse twice . . .

7 . . . like this. Fold A across to the right

8 Tuck the nearside top quarter into the boat. Take it over the top of A, but not over the top of the reverse fold layers at the bow (front) . . .

9 . . . like this. Similarly, fold in the far side layer, but this time also folding it over the reverse at the bow to close it shut. Flatten the bottom of the boat.

10 The Rowing Boat complete.

ROSETTE

Another design by the author. The idea is a development from a known fan lock, but here done twice between Steps 7–10, once either side of the centre. The result is Step 11, which was then found to "snap" open obligingly to hold a satisfying circular shape under tension. For storage it can be collapsed flat back to Step 10! Use an oblong of medium-weight paper, twice as long as it is wide – for instance 4 × 8 in (10 × 20 cm).

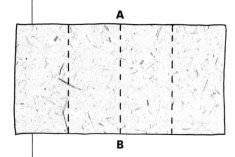

1 Valley fold into quarters. Note A and B.

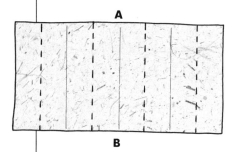

2 Valley fold into eighths.

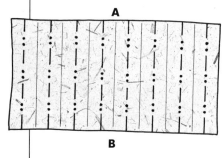

3 Place mountains between the valleys, so that . . .

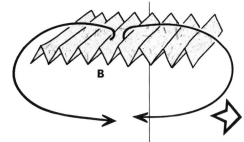

4 . . . the folds concertina together. Unfold the central crease AB.

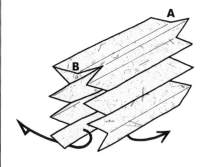

5 Unfold the first crease at each end of the pleats . . .

6 . . . like this. Squash the pleats flat. Turn over.

7 Fold in half. Note CD.

8 Allow the pleats to cascade open between A and B, but hold the central layers flat at C and D. At the right, turn in the corners with valley folds. At the left, do the same, but with mountain folds.

9 At the right, valley the projecting pleat into the line of pleats. At the left, do the same, but with a mountain fold.

10 Spread AB apart.

11 Make a straight mountain fold connecting AEB. This will "snap" the rosette into its final shape. Be forceful!

12 The Rosette complete.